A PASSION
FOR THE GOSPEL

A PASSION
FOR THE GOSPEL

Confessing Jesus Christ
for the 21st Century

Mark Achtemeier
Andrew Purves
editors

Geneva Press
Louisville, Kentucky

Acknowledgments will be found on page xii.

Book design by Sharon Adams
Cover design by Dean Nicklas

First edition

Published by Geneva Press
Louisville, Kentucky

This book is printed on acid-free paper that meets the American National Standards Institute Z39.48 standard. ∞

PRINTED IN THE UNITED STATES OF AMERICA

00 01 02 03 04 05 06 07 08 09 — 10 9 8 7 6 5 4 3 2 1

Library of Congress Cataloging-in-Publication Data

A catalog record for this book is available from the Library of Congress.
ISBN 0-664-50128-1

Contents

Dedicated to
Professor John H. Leith,
Theologian, Churchman,
and Defender of the Reformed Faith

‡ ‡ ‡ ‡ ‡

Introduction

This book represents voices of a movement that is presently exerting significant influence within the life of North American Presbyterianism. This movement is characterized by a number of perspectives. Among these are a deep sense of the authority of scripture, the conviction that God calls us to a personal holiness that includes sexual purity, and an abiding concern for the renewal of the church on the basis of the historical doctrines and practices of the Christian faith interpreted within the Reformed tradition. Yet these perspectives do not adequately define what is really at the center. The thread uniting every contribution in this book is the unambiguous confession of the unique, singular, saving Lordship of Jesus Christ.

Every writer holds to this center of the evangelical theology of the Reformation and the classical Trinitarian faith of the church: Jesus is Lord. They may not agree on all matters of Christian doctrine and life, but they do agree on this, that there is salvation in no other name under heaven than the name of Jesus Christ (Acts 4:12). It is shared clarity and conviction concerning this central confession that gives this book its fundamental coherence and that defines the movement of which each contributor is a part.

All Christians, of course, confess that Jesus is Lord. One would hardly be a Christian otherwise. We cannot assume, however, that this confession means the same thing to every Christian. Thus the movement represented by this book stands in contrast to other points of view, other ways of understanding the meaning of Jesus' Lordship. There is a tendency today on the part of some people to distill the gospel into principles, into abstract concepts that begin to function on their own as the real content of the faith. Thus we hear much talk of justice, inclusivity, hospitality, love, and so on. These are all virtuous themes. While they have a legitimate rootage in Jesus' ministry, and, indeed, in biblical theology in general, such conceptual abstractions have a way of breaking free from their roots in scripture and receiving their essential definitions and content from sources other than the Bible. In so doing they tend to assume an independent character that allows them to be turned back in criticism against scripture and Christian tradition, frequently on behalf of culturally determined causes and agendas. The problem here is the elevation of an abstract Christ-principle or visionary ideal that replaces the person of Jesus Christ and our union with Christ as the basis for the Christian life. Where classical faith calls believers to a participation in God's life and mission by an exclusive attachment to the Person of Jesus Christ, which is the work of the Holy Spirit, the modernist tendency is to call for an adherence to only the ideas of Jesus. This is not wrong in itself, but it represents a diminished view of Christian faith and one that is very vulnerable to being co-opted by various cultural agendas.

The authors of the essays and sermons published here believe that, at its roots, Christian faith is not characterized by a passion for an ethical vision (although that is most decidedly included), but by a passion for a Person—the Person of Jesus Christ, who is the gospel. The Christian life is not a religious abstraction representing the ideas of Jesus but a living relationship with him and, through him, with the Father.

This book, through the twenty contributions, affirms that by a singular confession of and an exclusive attachment to Jesus Christ our Lord, through our union with him, we share in his life before God and in his mission from God. In presenting various aspects of this theme, the book follows the basic pattern of "Union in Christ: A Declaration for the Church." This declaration of faith was commissioned by the Presbyterian Coalition—a federation of evangelical and renewal groups within the PC(USA)—and ratified in October 1998. Not all of the authors contributing to this volume are self-identified with the

Presbyterian Coalition as an organization, nor is what follows a strict commentary on the "Union in Christ" declaration. But the essays and sermons are grounded in the basic theology contained therein. This theology is traditional, yet written for today. It is missional, for it begins with God's mission to and for the world in and through Jesus Christ, which divine mission constrains and compels the mission of the church. So stated, it is Trinitarian, for the whole of Christian life is understood as given from the Father, through the Son, in the power of the Holy Spirit, and responding to the Father, through the Son, in the power of the Holy Spirit. In this way, what follows is the faith of the church catholic, at least as Reformed Christians of an evangelical persuasion understand it.

We express our appreciation to the contributors to this volume. Without exception, our authors wrote under constraints of time that were very demanding. We are deeply grateful for their commitment to this book and for the quality of their work. It is our earnest prayer that what follows will both bless all who read it and advance the quality of theological conversation within the church.

Mark Achtemeier

Andrew Purves

NOTE

1. For a copy of the Declaration, a statement of its origins, and an explanation of its content, see Andrew Purves and Mark Achtemeier, *Union in Christ: A Declaration for the Church* (Louisville, Ky.: Witherspoon Press, 1999).

Acknowledgments

Scripture quotations from the Revised Standard Version of the Bible (RSV) are copyright © 1989 by the Divison of Christian Education of the National Council of the Churches of Christ in the U.S.A. and are used by permission.

Scripture quotations from the New Revised Standard Version of the Bible (NRSV) are copyright © 1989 by the Division of Christian Education of the National Council of the Churches of Christ in the U.S.A. and are used by permission.

Scripture quotations from the New International Version of the Bible (NIV) are copyright © 1973, 1978, 1984 International Bible Society. Used by permission of Zondervan Bible Publishers.

Scripture quotations marked (PTN) are from Eugene H. Peterson, *The Message: The New Testament in Contemporary English* (Colorado Springs: NavPress, 1993), copyright 1993. All rights reserved.

Scripture quotations marked (NLT) are taken from the *Holy Bible, New Living Translation*, copyright © 1996. Used by permission of Tyndale House Publishers, Inc., Wheaton, Illinois 60189. All rights reserved.

"Last Kiss," by Wayne Cochran, is © 1961 (Renewed) Trio Music Company, Inc., Fort Knox Music, Inc. All rights reserved. Used by permission.

Contributors

Editors

P. Mark Achtemeier
Assistant Professor of Systematic Theology
University of Dubuque Theological Seminary

Andrew Purves
Hugh Thomson Kerr Associate Professor of Pastoral Theology
Pittsburgh Theological Seminary

Contributors

Elizabeth Achtemeier
Adjunct Professor of Bible and Homiletics, retired
Union Theological Seminary in Virginia

M. Craig Barnes
Pastor, The National Presbyterian Church
Washington, D.C.

Peter B. Barnes
Pastor, First Presbyterian Church
Boulder, Colorado

B. Clayton Bell, Sr.
Pastor, Highland Park Presbyterian Church
Dallas, Texas

Jeffrey Francis Bullock
President and Professor of Hermeneutics and Homiletics
University of Dubuque Theological Seminary

Stephen D. Crocco
James Lenox Librarian
Princeton Theological Seminary

Theresa Ip Froehlich
Member-at-large
Presbytery of North Puget Sound

Sherron George
Assistant Professor of Evangelism and Mission
Austin Presbyterian Theological Seminary

Jack Haberer
Pastor, Clear Lake Presbyterian Church
Houston, Texas

James H. Logan, Jr.
Pastor, South Tryon Presbyterian Church
Charlotte, North Carolina

Mary Holder Naegeli
Pastor, First Presbyterian Church
Concord, California

Earl F. Palmer
Pastor, University Presbyterian Church
Seattle, Washington

Charles Partee
P. C. Rossin Professor of Church History
Pittsburgh Theological Seminary

Margaret Kim Peterson
Assistant Professor of Theological Studies
Eastern College, St. Davids, Pennsylvania

Catherine J. S. Purves
Pastor, Bellevue United Presbyterian Church
Bellevue, Pennsylvania

Joseph B. Rightmyer
Executive Director
Presbyterians for Renewal

James M. Singleton, Jr.
Pastor, Covenant Presbyterian Church
Austin, Texas

Scott W. Sunquist
W. Don McClure Associate Professor of World Mission and Evangelism
Pittsburgh Theological Seminary

PART 1

Confessing
Jesus Christ

The Gospel of Jesus Christ

Scott W. Sunquist

So do not be ashamed to testify about our Lord, or ashamed of me his prisoner. But join with me in suffering for the gospel by the power of God, who has saved us and called us to a holy life—not because of anything we have done, but because of his own purpose and grace. This grace was given us in Christ Jesus before the beginning of time.

—2 Timothy 1:8–9, NIV

The power of the gospel surprises us. When I was teaching at a theological college in Singapore, I was surprised, and also flattered, that the students invited me to play on the college soccer team. Our first game was against a newer team made up of young men living at a Christian halfway house for former drug addicts. Most had been gang members or members of local Chinese triad societies. There were Tamil Indians, Chinese, and Malay. As we lined up for the kickoff, I looked across at my midfield opponent and noticed that he appeared to be wearing tight black and red pants. Upon closer inspection I could see that he was not wearing pants, but his legs were replete with tattoos from hip to heel. He was missing teeth, and in general he looked as if he cared far more about the outcome of this "friendly match" than I. It was a very difficult two-hour match. When the final whistle was blown, the theological college had been soundly beaten by the former addicts.

After a match, we usually lined up and shook hands. This time everyone hugged all the others and said things like, "Praise Jesus . . . Glory to Jesus. . . ." We were overwhelmed by the praise and encouraging comments that flowed from the lips of those who had just crushed us. Our opponents were very skilled, hard-working people who had become loving evangelists for the kingdom of God. As one of our student players, who volunteered at the halfway house, remarked, "Now that is the power of the gospel." And so it is.

The gospel is a type of shorthand used by the biblical writers for the heart of the Christian message. The gospel, in a person, is Jesus Christ. The gospel, in a phrase, is the salvific work of God the Father through Jesus Christ in the power of the Holy Spirit for the whole world. But when we have said this, we have only given the shorthand for the cosmic work of salvation that God has accomplished though Jesus Christ. The gospel is a good word (news) for all of creation. "In the beginning was the Word, and the Word was with God, and the Word was God. He was with God in the beginning" (John 1:1, NIV). The good word from God has existed from before creation, is the head over all of creation, and is the Lord over the new creation. God's word and act are always before us, meaning both in front of us and prior to our words and acts.

We are always responding to God's primary *word-act* in Jesus Christ. This presupposes that Jesus Christ is God speaking and acting for us in the space-time continuum. The gospel is therefore the power of God in human history to transform and redeem that history. The cosmic redemption is founded upon a specific Jewish peasant killed as a common criminal who was buried and rose from the dead to live eternally. Jesus, the word-act of God, is the gospel of God.

Gospel Confusion

Words on one level are merely lines, curves, and dots upon a page that may evoke strong emotions even from the most reasonable of people. My mother, for example, has a different response to the word *gay* than my children do. There is a similar confusion of emotional responses today to the word *gospel*. Some Christians will instruct their young adults as they go off to college, "Be sure to find a good church that preaches the gospel!" Other Christian parents will tell their children not to get caught up in some "gospel church," as if it may be a type of authoritarian cult. Some preachers will tell you with a gently understated pride that they preach only the gospel: "Every Sunday my congregation gets the gospel!" Other preachers will avoid at all costs the term *gospel* in describing their preaching. *Gospel* is an older term, they reason, associated with outdated revivalist and imperialistic missionary approaches.

Let us be honest and admit that the term *gospel* has been taken over by the more fundamentalist, or at least by more conservative, denominations. In the mainline churches we have not fought to reclaim this important term that is used to summarize the message of God's saving work in the world. We need to be very intentional in reclaiming the use of the word *gospel* for our churches. Why should we care? The word *gospel* (*euangelion/ euangelizomai:* good news/evangelize) is used 138 times in the New Testament, usually to summarize the work and message of Jesus Christ. If we do not reclaim the term, then *gospel* will suffer further narrowing (e.g., to mean only individual salvation), and before we know it, we will have lost an important theological concept. What may soon follow is that we will surrender other important terms (Jesus, kingdom, Father) because we do not like the way others use the words. As our theological vocabulary becomes impoverished by partisan erosion, we will lose some of the breadth of our own theological discourse and be forced into a theological backwater. The breadth of theological vocabulary gives expression to the breadth and depth of God's work in the world.

Already the term *gospel* has taken on a more limited and partisan usage today. In an effort to reclaim some of the rich meaning of the gospel, we will look at the gospel from four perspectives: the heart of the gospel, the extent of the gospel, the power of the gospel, and, finally, the meaning of the gospel. It is this author's sincere prayer that such a presentation will aid in recovering the use of the word *gospel* for the ecumenical church.

The Heart of the Gospel

The gospel is the good news *of* (about/concerning) Jesus Christ. When Philip took time to explain the good news (from Isaiah) to an Ethiopian, he "told him the good news about Jesus" (Acts 8:35, NIV). The heart of the gospel is contained in the history of this one man, Jesus, and the interpretation of his life. It is not just that a peasant Jew was born, wandered around teaching, and was killed. This would be just another tragedy of our fallen world, where the poor are oppressed and justice still waits its time. But the heart of the gospel is that Jesus, God *with* us, died for *our* sins and was raised from the dead, conquering both sin and death. The historical "facts" themselves need interpretation. "Therefore, my brothers and sisters, I want you to know that *through Jesus* the forgiveness of sins is proclaimed to you. Through him everyone who believes is justified from everything you could not be justified from by the law of Moses" (Acts 13:38–39, NIV). Such summaries of the gospel are given by Luke, Peter, Paul, and John as a type of shorthand: Jesus Christ conquered sin, injustice, oppression, and death by himself being raised from the dead. It is good news because what we needed to do, but could not do, has been done for us. We have received salvation when we deserved condemnation. We have been justified when we could not justify ourselves.

This good news of salvation is revealed in the cross. The cross shows forth the greatness of God's grace and the height of human pride and rebellion. In the cross, death was killed, and humble submission conquered worldly power. In the violent and political act of an official execution, the oppressed have been released, hearts of stone have become hearts of flesh, and peace and justice have embraced.

At this point we must acknowledge that this victory was not just a literary, mythic, or imaginary victory. This is much more than the victory expressed in wishful thinking of the sort that says, "Imagine yourself released from your cocoon and flying like a butterfly!" No, wishful thinking and empty words are not enough. This is a real victory, and it has been made known through the empty tomb. Injustice and death did all they could to silence God's Word, but his victory over death reveals that sin, suffering, and death have been conquered. Again, this is far more than a religious ascent to a higher level of consciousness that escapes the hard realities of the physical world. In Jesus' resurrection we see that God takes our real, gutsy, dirty, and oppressive reality seriously. God does not merely say, "Think peaceful thoughts." In the resurrection of the body, God says, "Yes, real liberation in this life of blood, sweat, and tears is accomplished." Those who are "in Christ" and have experienced the pain, suffering, and injustices of this world know that suffering does not have the last word. God has spoken, and God has acted with effectiveness in the history of humankind. This is the heart of the gospel.

The Extent of the Gospel

This good news is for all: every person and all peoples. Any description of the gospel that does not include all peoples, nations, tribes, and languages is not the gospel of Jesus Christ. On the one hand, this inclusive nature of the gospel brings persecution. Inclusivity brings persecution because the absolute and inclusive claims of the gospel are a threat to other powers and authorities who have a great stake in preserving the boundaries that define the scope of their own rule and dominion. Those who are united with Christ disregard such boundaries, giving witness to all people. This may raise the anger and hostility of others. Christians are persecuted because of their witness more than because of their worship.

On the other hand, this inclusive nature of the gospel is often misunderstood as pluralism. It is taken to mean that since the gospel is meant for all, all then are saved either consciously or unconsciously through the work of the gospel. But the inclusivity of the gospel of Jesus Christ is not the cheap grace of pluralism.

A pluralistic type of inclusiveness that ignores the shape and character of people's actual response to God undermines the dignity of the human will, which is part of the image of God that is regenerated in redemption. It also falls into the trap of interpreting the gospel primarily as a matter of individual salvation. The gospel concerns much more than individuals being saved. It concerns also the kingdom of God, the fulfillment of God's loving intention for the whole cosmos, which is like a mustard seed, a lost coin, a banquet, the rich becoming poor, and the poor being lifted up. The gospel is a costly inclusion rooted in the obedience of the Son and proclaimed by the witness of those who are in Christ. Only in Christ are sinful human beings included in the kingdom, which is open to all and intended for all.

The inclusive nature of the gospel means that Jesus' life, death, and resurrection are meant for all peoples, no matter where they may be, what language they may speak, or what they may worship at the present. In this sense, the gospel is universal. It is meant for western materialists, Kurdish refugees, and Tibetan Buddhists. To withhold the gospel from any people is to deny the essence of the gospel as universal. Throughout the history of the church this inclusivity has been a threat to governments and self-maintained groupings of people. The gospel is not bound by any culture or defined by any language, government, or economic system. When Christians insist on giving a witness to the love of God in Christ, or speaking up about the justice and the righteousness of God, people in power who are challenged by the teaching resist the good news. This has always been the case.

We know from the New Testament record that the universality or inclusiveness of the gospel has been one of the greatest stumbling blocks to belief. From Jesus' first sermon at Nazareth recorded by Luke to the final revelation of the heavenly kingdom in Revelation, all people are to be included in the kingdom of God. Of special note is Luke's description of the memorable address Jesus gave at his inaugural lecture in his hometown synagogue (Luke 4:14–50). In good Jewish fashion Jesus selected a popular text from the prophet Isaiah (our chapter 61) describing the Lord's jubilee and liberation for his people. His synagogue worshipers loved it. Then he encouraged their support even further when he said to them, "Today this scripture is fulfilled in your hearing" (v. 21, NIV). These oppressed Jews loved the young, local preacher. But this "good news for the poor," the proclamation of "freedom for the prisoners and the recovery of sight for the blind," even the "release [of] the oppressed," was not the full extent of the good news. Jesus made it clear, from the Jewish scriptures themselves, that this good news, which was being fulfilled in his person, was meant for all people. It was not the Israelites, but a Sidonian woman in Zarephath who received God's grace (v. 26). Again, Israelites were bypassed in the time of Elisha the prophet, and only a Syrian army commander was healed (v. 27). The gospel meaning is for all, or it has no gospel meaning at all. It is not the gospel if it is only for Jews, white Americans, and African Americans. The gospel must not be bound. Thus, they tried to kill Jesus, and eventually they succeeded.

Jesus gave new meaning to the reign of God. All people are to be included in the kingdom of righteousness. All people are to be received and transformed. Drug addicts, Chinese gang members, and American business executives are to be received and transformed by the gospel of God. It is a great paradox that those who seem furthest from God's righteousness in Jesus Christ are actually closest. When we exclude people from the witness of the gospel because they have another religion or another language or a different economic status, we are excluding ourselves. We are far from God's righteousness because we hold back the gospel from those different from ourselves. Such was the case of the Pharisees, and such is our great temptation today. The gospel of righteousness is for all, or it is not a gospel of righteousness at all.

The Power of the Gospel

Because the power of the gospel is from God, it is greater than anything in creation. The opening verses from 2 Timothy noted that this gospel is from the "power of God" and was given "before the beginning of time." We must not be deluded into underestimating the power of the gospel. The gospel's power transcends time: there is a past, present, and future reality to the gospel's power. It is from before the beginning of time, it is saving and reconciling today, and it will bring forth the new heaven and the new earth. The incarnation, resurrection, and ascension of Jesus Christ have been a display of the eternal power of God on our behalf. The word-act of Jesus Christ was in time, but it was for all of eternity.

In addition, this powerful work of God is a righteous and ethical work. The opening verses from 2 Timothy stated that this gospel "has saved us and called us to a holy life." These two aspects (salvation and sanctification) cannot be separated. God's power is revealed in weakness, and God's righteousness is revealed in humility. This is gospel or kingdom ethics. One of the greatest powers in this fallen world is death, and it is conquered through submission. Another great power, sin, is conquered through death, the very thing that sin produces. Thus, we are given in the gospel story the model for gospel transformation or sanctification. Those who would save their life must lose their life. For a seed of human life to grow, it must first die to self.

The power of gospel life and transformation travels through the lifeblood of humility and submission. This does not mean that the gospel is really a message of martyrdom and self-flagellation. In our submission and humility the power of God for the world is revealed. Power is revealed and made available for others in our personal weakness. Recall the soccer match described at the beginning of this chapter. Each of these former drug addicts came to a point of surrender of personal will before being transformed by the power of the gospel. This was the testimony of each player after our game. It is the same for each of us today. The power for us to be transformed and to be transforming agents comes through our own humility, confession, and repentance. It is the purpose of the gospel to transform, but the pathway of transformation is through humility.

A discussion about the gospel's power must include the relationship between power and suffering. Again, in our passage from 2 Timothy, Paul reminds us that receiving the gospel can be more than a little embarrassing. Christians follow a man killed as a criminal, and Paul himself was in prison. So Paul tells the believers not to be ashamed, but to "join with me in suffering for the gospel" (v. 8, NIV). On one level the good news of salvation comes to us through suffering—the sufferings of Jesus Christ—and on another level our reception and understanding of the gospel will also come through suffering. Victory is still present in the gospel, but in the mystery of the Trinity this victory is revealed through suffering.

I remember a church leader who made a quick evaluation of a younger minister, saying, "His problem is that he has not suffered." It wasn't until years later that I understood the wisdom of that statement and how much that evaluation came from the heart and the power of the gospel. "Blessed are those who mourn, for they will be comforted" (Matt. 5:4, NIV). The power of the gospel is released as we "know Christ and the power of his resurrection and the fellowship of sharing in his sufferings." God's power to redeem did not come as God bypassed suffering and death, but redemption came as God walked directly into that valley of shadows that is suffering and death. As a result, suffering is redeemed by the very power of God. In a world of great oppression and suffering, it is good news that suffering is redeemed by God's mighty work through Jesus Christ, the "Man of Sorrows."

The Meaning of the Gospel

We can never fully grasp the meaning of the gospel for the world. When we say this, we need to keep in mind that we can say—and have said—something about the heart, extent, and power of the gospel, even if the full meaning eludes us. There are three major reasons that the unfolding meaning of the gospel is always before us.

First, the meaning of the gospel is constantly unfolding as the work of God the Father, in Jesus the Son, is applied, through the work of the Holy Spirit, in different places and times. What the gospel means to poor peasant farmers in Columbia is not the same as, but neither is it unrelated to, what it means to Dalits in India, or Dayaks in Malaysia. For all of these people, the gospel of Jesus Christ comes to shatter old idols and liberate individuals and cultures to serve the true God. But for the Colombian farmer that gospel liberation will be quite different than for the Dalit or the Dayak. By its very nature, the gospel is both universal and particular. The gospel takes on the particular cultural expression and speaks to the particular needs. Some give witness to the coming of the gospel saying that they were freed from the power of the spirits of the ancestors. For others the gospel came and liberated the poor from oppression and hunger. Others have been liberated from the idolatry of materialism or from bondage to alcohol. All, however, are giving testimony to the heart of the gospel, the work of Jesus Christ for the redemption of creation.

Second, we see the unfolding meaning of the gospel in the various responses to its presentation. What is good news from God is not received as good news by all. The gospel that unites is the same gospel that divides. New Testament theologian Joachim Jeremias has noted that the good news divides the spirits. People have always responded to the good news in one of two ways: repentance or rejection. The good news itself reveals what is central to a person's or culture's existence. "Because the gospel offers the greatest salvation, at the same time it can bring about the greatest disaster. Guilt arises from grace."[1] Thus, there will be different meanings to the gospel for an individual or a culture as the gospel brings to light the need for grace, and then the work of grace. Those who reject the need will not receive what is needed. In this sense we can understand Jesus' cryptic saying, "I did not come to bring peace, but a sword" (Matt. 10:34, NIV). The gospel of peace, in almost every context, is also the gospel of the sword. The gospel cuts out that which is lethal (sin) and separates people according to loyalties.

Third, the meaning of the gospel is ever unfolding because it is the gospel both of the kingdom announced and of behavior renounced. Earlier we looked at a summary statement of Jesus' message in Luke 4. The opening of Mark's Gospel gives another type of summary statement of Jesus' ministry. "After John was put in prison, Jesus went into Galilee proclaiming the good news of God. 'The time has come,' he said. 'The kingdom of God is near. Repent and believe the good news!' " (Mark 1:15, NIV). Again, Jesus' message is basically good news being announced, but in this passage, a call to repentance (renouncing) is given along with the announcement of the kingdom. Both the call and the announcement are part of the gospel. There is a clear call to life based upon a call to believe. Believing and doing are of the same fabric. The word-act that is Jesus' life and ministry is to be reflected in us as we put on Christ. We are to believe and so act. We are to repent, or turn away from certain behaviors, and then believe the gospel of the kingdom. What we renounce, however, is as varied as are the cultures and people who witness the good news. The gospel means that some renounce certain behaviors or thoughts that others have never even considered.

I was once leading a small group in Singapore made up mostly of fairly wealthy Singaporeans, along with one Filipino woman who had come from a conservative student ministry in the Philippines. As we went around the room sharing prayer requests, the more modern and sophisticated Singaporeans shared about spiritual needs (e.g., greater love for God, knowing God's guidance), and then the Filipino woman talked about her counseling center in northern Luzon for liberation fighters and their families. The room was silent. The rest of the group could not imagine that this quiet, little Filipino friend was training to provide pastoral counseling for liberation fighters! For her the gospel meant repenting of her smug and polite attitudes that did not take the sufferings of her people seriously. The gospel of grace had transformed her belief and her life. Her repentance was very hard for middle-class, urban, cosmopolitan Singaporeans to understand. Our understanding of the meaning of the gospel was far bigger after a few weeks of discussing the oppression and poverty of the Philippines. We all came to understand more completely how the good news of Jesus Christ receives us by grace and sanctifies us by the very power of God. It is not possible to believe in this gospel without letting it change your life.

Conversely, it is not possible to change your life without a change in belief. Repent and believe.

The power of the gospel does surprise us. It surprises us in who the persons are whom it redeems and transforms. It surprises us in how individuals and cultures are transformed. And the gospel surprises in when individuals and nations (*ethne*) are transformed. In this sense the meaning of the gospel is always before us as we live in joyful thanksgiving for what God has done and is doing through Jesus Christ. But we are "not like those without hope," for "while we were yet sinners, Christ died for us" (Rom. 5:8, RSV). Thus "we know, brothers [and sisters], loved by God, that he has chosen you, because our gospel came to you not simply with words, but also with power and the Holy Spirit and with deep conviction" (1 Thess. 1:4–5a, NIV). For this we are thankful, and we stand in awe.

NOTE

1. Joachim Jeremias, *New Testament Theology* (New York: Charles Scribner's Sons, 1971), 121.

The Lordship of Jesus Christ

Mark Achtemeier

"Jesus is Lord." The phrase stands as one of the simplest and earliest confessions of Christian faith found in the scripture (e.g., Phil 2:11; Acts 2:36; John 20:28; Col. 2:6). It is a simple phrase and yet so utterly profound that no one can confess it truly, according to the apostle Paul, apart from the active working of the Holy Spirit (1 Cor. 12:3).

Many of us tend to overlook or short-circuit the depth and profundity of this confession in the frequently overheated atmosphere of contemporary church debates. On the theological right, one sometimes finds "Jesus is Lord" understood as the working equivalent of, say, "Jesus is the Boss." Jesus being Boss, of course, means that Jesus sets the Rules (such assertion is frequently accompanied by waving about the Authority of Scripture as a kind of battle flag). And "Jesus sets the Rules" means that all those nefarious rule-breakers out there (who are obviously none other than our own ecclesiastical opponents) are in *very big trouble!*

On the theological left, one often finds the Lordship of Christ warmly embraced. But this embrace frequently serves as the authorizing warrant for attitudes and values that, while claiming some legitimate rootage in Jesus' ministry, quickly take on a life

15

of their own. This can happen to such an extent that we soon find them turned back in critique against the very biblical text that gave them birth, usually in defense of values or behaviors that progressive opinion would like to protect from scriptural assault. *Inclusiveness, liberation, justice,* and even *love* come to mind as concepts that in recent memory have taken on such elastic qualities, becoming tools by which we may critique certain portions of scripture that we find uncomfortable or offensive. Perhaps more to the point, they have become tools by which we may critique those regressive-minded ecclesiastical opponents of ours who insist on taking the scriptures "literally!"

In both cases, of course, the Lordship of Christ has been replaced by a lordship of abstract ideas—of disembodied rules and commandments on the one hand, and free-floating moral abstractions on the other. Jesus the Jew, the shockingly offensive and surpassingly mysterious denizen of a Roman-occupied Palestine two thousand years distant, has retreated safely into the background, and we in the church are left to squabble with one another over the implementation of our own vastly more congenial and conventional decrees and concepts.

In this essay we will try to make a start at repenting of our religious abstractions. Along the way we hope to catch a glimpse of some implications of Jesus' Lordship when the "Jesus" in question is not merely a symbolic representative of our cherished values and ideals, but the One to whom the apostolic witness points across the centuries of the church's existence. To keep ourselves honest in this endeavor, we will organize our discussion around three identifying affirmations that will help ensure that the Jesus of our ecclesiastical conversations is the very same Jesus to whom the apostolic church bears witness. In short, (1) the Jesus whose Lordship we confess is the Incarnate Word, the only begotten Son of God, present among us in human flesh; (2) he is the Crucified One, condemned to death under Pontius Pilate, who died and was buried; and (3) he is the Risen and Ascended One, who was raised on the third day and will come again in glory to usher in the fullness of God's reign. These three affirmations mark the "Jesus" we are considering as the Jesus whom the apostles proclaimed. What are some of the implications of confessing *this* Jesus as Lord?

The Lordship of the Incarnate Word

"For in him all the fullness of God was pleased to dwell." (Col. 1:19, NRSV)

"Whoever has seen me has seen the Father." (John 14:9, NRSV)

The one true God has come among us as a human being. That is the astounding claim that forms the center of the apostles' preaching, and indeed that the apostolic community attributes to Jesus' own witness concerning himself. Jesus, the son of Mary, is not a divine prophet, not a spiritual genius, not a high and noble ethical example, but God himself, mysteriously and wholly present to us as this one human being, while never ceasing to be always and at the same time fully and completely God. The living God has invaded the precincts of time and history, and nothing will ever be the same again.

Christ's Lordship is thus inseparable from this claim that Jesus is God. *Kyrios*, the New Testament word for "Lord," translates the Hebrew *YHWH* or *adonai*—the traditional Old Testament designation for God. In Trinitarian terms, we indeed say that we confess Jesus as Lord when the Spirit opens our eyes to recognize the glory of the Father in Jesus the Son.

The presence with us of the incarnate Lord of the church shifts forever the foundation of the church's life and worship away from human ideals, aspirations, and achievements to *what God has done*. Repenting of all the frenetic busyness by which we seek to justify ourselves, the church stands in mute silence, wonder, and adoration before this truth of all truths, that *the Word became flesh and dwelt among us*. In particular, the Lordship of Christ the incarnate Word frees us among other things from the spiritual and religious tyranny of our own feelings, projects, and subjective opinions. Let us elaborate briefly on each of these.

Against the Lordship of Our Feelings

Worship so easily becomes focused on us rather than God. Almost without realizing it, we lapse into identifying Christian faith with our own inward religious feelings, attitudes, and experiences. Much worship in this and every age finds its goal, not in the praise and adoration of the triune God that is our perpetual joy and duty, but in the provision of a "meaningful experience" for the assembled congregation. What we do on Sunday morning is properly directed toward the praise of God. The first purpose of worship is not to conjure up an emotional excitement, to provide the requisite helpings of (spiritual!) amusement and inspiration, garnished perhaps with a few nuggets of satisfying, commonsense wisdom—all in order to keep the gathered assembly engaged and entertained. The center of the faith is not what we do, or think, or feel. The center is rather *what God has done*, coming among us in Jesus Christ.

In the face of such temptations to put ourselves rather than God at the center of our worship, we must proclaim insistently and persistently that the liberating message of God's ongoing saving activity in the world by the power of the Spirit is not tied to our adrenaline levels. Salvation does not depend on the state of our feelings. Christ continues to be Lord and Head of the church even among worshipers who are bored, depressed, or anxious. Our perpetual obsessions with psychic and physiological states receive an utterly gracious contradiction and overturning in the invitation of the incarnate Word, who delivers the kingdom to persons "poor in spirit" (Matt. 5:3).

This is not of course an argument for boring, uninspiring worship, nor is the point to reduce our praise of God to some lukewarm, purely intellectual enterprise. It *is* an argument for worship that seeks first Christ's kingdom and Christ's righteousness, that has its focus in God and not in us, and that waits upon the divine good pleasure to add all these other things as well. Christ is Lord, to be worshiped, feared, honored, and obeyed—regardless of the status of our "experiences"!

Against the Lordship of Our Programs

The confession of Christ's Lordship also undermines every attempt to transmute Christian hope into this-worldly reliance upon the ultimate success of our own church programs, projects, and reforms, however noble and well intentioned they may be. Fashionable theological opinion in recent decades has all too often assumed a dichotomy between the church's otherworldly "spiritual" concerns, and its vastly more relevant this-worldly strivings toward justice and liberation and service of all kinds to people in need. "The world sets the agenda for the church" has been one of the popular slogans embodying this point of view. At the local level, such thinking has translated into the practical assumption that the church exists in order to meet people's "needs." Such an assumption proves an extremely harsh taskmaster, because the reality of the fallen human heart is that people's felt needs have a way of increasing without limit. This false lordship of our own programs and projects takes a devastating toll in clergy burnout as the demands for services and multidisciplinary expertise multiply endlessly. Smaller congregations who simply lack the resources to "compete" effectively in the demanding marketplace for the provision of religious goods and services become demoralized..

Beneath all of this well-meaning but increasingly frantic busyness of the churches, one detects a modern variant of the age-old attempt on the part of human beings to justify ourselves. We build our towers up to heaven and make a great name for ourselves. We hope to secure the foundations of our existence by the work of our own hands. What a note of grace and liberation it is, then, to be reminded of the Lordship of Jesus Christ. The church is here—and deserves to be here!—not because of what *we* are doing but because Christ has called us out into community. I saw this gracious recognition embodied in very practical terms one time in a tiny rural church in the middle of an isolated, wind-swept plain. This congregation was not in a position to offer lots of programs—their meager resources were barely sufficient to keep the doors open on Sunday mornings. But what they *could* offer was eloquently stated in a sign out front: "Join us for communion this Sunday, and receive Jesus Christ." The church lives not by what we are able to do, but by what God has done and continues to do in Jesus Christ by the power of the Holy Spirit!

What then of our projects and programs? Listen again to Jesus' words: "Those who want to save their life will lose it, and those who lose their life for my sake will find it" (Matt. 16.25, NRSV). As we cease to make these things the justifying reason for our existence as a church, as we hand over our false identification of the success of these programs with the reality of God's working in the world, as we renounce the false lordship of our own efforts, we receive them back in a new and gracious form. Where once there was compulsion and a certain grim, self-righteous determination, there emerges now the joyful freedom of the children of God! Once there was desperate struggle to *deserve* our existence before God and to earn our place in the social order, with everything riding on the success of our efforts. In the light of Christ's Lordship there now emerge thanksgiving, praise, and gratitude for what God has done. Perhaps we may even find the freedom to experiment, to take risks, to be profligate in loving, to embrace hopeless causes—all as sign and witness and celebration that in the light of Christ's Lordship no expression of love is ever finally hopeless or pointless.

Against the Lordship of Our Religious Opinions

"If you had known me, you would have known my Father also; henceforth you know him and have seen him" (John 14:7, RSV). In Jesus Christ, the Word made flesh, we have true and reliable knowledge of God and of God's claim upon us. That assertion collides with the deepest instincts of our secularized culture. In two areas especially is this collision acute.

First, American secular culture has tried very hard to remove religious claims from the realm of truth. "Facts," the stuff of which real truth is composed, are entirely different things—so the story goes—from "values," which are matters of individual preference. Religion, of course, is the prime example of a "value." Questions about the truth or falsehood of particular religious claims are thus declared to be category mistakes, as nonsensical as questions about the truth or falsehood of the color of the socks one chooses to wear. This assumption is fiercely guarded and enforced by the culture that, one suspects, doesn't want to hear about a Lord who stands in judgment over it. Thus, any person making substantive, religiously grounded truth claims in a way that commands public attention is quickly labeled with the severest terms of moral opprobrium of which our secularized society is capable. Persons lifting up religious truth claims are denounced as bigoted, fanatical, intolerant, irrational, arrogant, fundamentalist, hate-filled, extremist—and the list goes on.

A second area where confession of Christ's Lordship collides with the worldview of secular culture is in the public/private distinction. Powerful forces in our society have attempted the removal of all religious claims and expressions from the public to the strictly private sphere. As a matter of personal "preference," religion is permitted to exercise limited claims over the private lives and activities of individual believers, in much the same way that I might personally resolve always to wear either black or brown socks to work. But as soon as religion begins making assertions about any reality or obligation that extends into the public sphere, societal condemnation is quick to follow. Suggestions that religiously grounded insights should help inform—or even have voice!—in debates over the shape of the national life, for instance, are quickly and vigorously denounced as intolerable violations of the so-called separation between church and state. Churches or religious organizations that press too insistently the notion that faith commitments have concrete implications for the way believers should participate in public political life can be faced with severe social sanctions, such as lawsuits and suspension of tax-exempt status.

Such cultural propaganda exacts a significant toll on the life and faith of Christian communities. New believers come into the church deeply suspicious of notions that Christian faith could be true in any sense that has implications beyond the realm of their own private feelings. The assumption that religious faith is a matter of essentially arbitrary personal choice makes church discipline, or even the cultivation of minimally coherent communities, extremely challenging. Public presentation of religion as a set of personal predilections on a par with, say, an interest in model trains, exerts a trivializing effect that undermines the habits and practices necessary to sustain persons in committed discipleship.

Over against all this the church has to claim ever anew the astonishing—and deeply offensive!—claims of Jesus Christ. "Whoever has seen me has seen the Father" (John 14:9, NRSV). Such a claim leaves little room for the "nice" teacher of uplifting—if ultimately innocuous—spiritual wisdom who regularly inhabits our culturally approved versions of pseudo-Christian piety. The man who could make such claims for himself would have to be, as C. S. Lewis pointed out, either a lunatic, a devil . . . or the incarnate Son of God.[1] Christ himself cuts off all other avenues of escape from his claims.

Confessing Christ the incarnate Lord, then, gives the church a solid anchor on which to found her life and hope, in the midst of the ever-shifting sands of religious opinion. In Christ we are given genuine knowledge of the Father, by the illumination of the Spirit. Such confession gives to the church boldness in the face of all the would-be lords of this world, and delivers us from their power to dictate the terms of our existence.

The principalities and powers of this world bitterly oppose such confession. They are happy to countenance a Lord over the private religious conscience of faithful believers and on occasion will even encourage such belief when it suits their purposes. But a King who is sovereign over all earthly kings and a living Lord who is destined to rule the heavens and the earth and all things visible and invisible, they are still inclined to crucify. Part of the challenge for the church, then, is learning to count the cost, to bear the public scandal, to claim the grace that allows us to shoulder our own crosses and to confess and follow this very Lord.

The Lordship of the Crucified Son of Man

"Now is the Son of Man glorified, and in him God is glorified." (John 13:31, RSV)

Jesus utters these words as his betrayer disappears into the night, setting finally in motion the events that will lead to his abandonment, suffering, and death on the cross. It is a staggering assertion, that *this* set of events should constitute his "glory." What are we to make of it, that this Lord establishes his reign precisely as he is lifted up on the cross of shame and death?

It means that Christ is determined to be Lord of and for *sinners*. "I came not to call the righteous, but sinners" (Matt. 9:13, RSV). As Jesus goes to the cross, he affirms and embraces in his own innocent person God's wrathful "No!" pronounced against all the sin and rebellion of our fallen humanity. In taking upon himself God's judgment against our sin, Jesus places himself in union and solidarity with sinners, making common cause with them, and praying for them even as they drive the spikes into his hands and feet. "[God] made him to be sin who knew no sin, so that in him we might become the righteousness of God" (2 Cor. 5:21, RSV).

The apostle Paul spins out the implications of all this in astonishing, and indeed shocking, fashion in his epistle to the Romans. The cross, says Paul, reveals God's wrathful rejection not of some sinful *portion* of humankind, not of the tares growing among the wheat, but of the whole of humanity. Jew and Greek, noble and ignoble (as judged from a human perspective), honorable and debased—"None is righteous, no, not one; no one understands, no one seeks for God. All have turned aside, together they have gone wrong; no one does good, not even one" (Rom. 3:10–12, RSV). All of our carefully crafted hierarchies of better and worse among human beings, every practical scale of respectable and not-so-respectable individuals, all the working distinctions we make between good church people and lost souls who earnestly need to repent, between doers of the law and those who despise it—everything is swept away in the fiery wrath of God's judgment as it is revealed and manifested in the cross.

Gone, too, are the schemes we concoct for justifying ourselves *part way*. Often the words "grace alone" on our lips signify a reliance on our own efforts to achieve a respectable and partially adequate job ascending the slopes of righteousness, all the while stipulating of course that it is God who provides the final boost needed to carry us over the summit. On the cross of Christ all such partial schemes are judged and exposed as rejections of the grace of God. "For there is no distinction; . . . all have sinned and fall short of the glory of God" (Rom. 3:22–23, RSV).

Why does God carry out this wholesale obliteration of our carefully crafted moral distinctions? Why this utterly sovereign disregard of all the critically important human differentiation between higher and lower, less and more, relatively better and relatively worse, upon which all of life and society and even religion itself are founded? By the cross God declares himself the enemy even of our all-important religious distinctions, casting the whole righteous and unrighteous edifice under judgment: "What then? Are we Jews any better off? No, not at all; for I have already charged that all men, both Jews and Greeks, are under the power of sin" (Rom. 3:9, RSV). Is this not a thoroughly contemptible exercise in throwing the baby out with the bath water, of burning the whole field for the sake of the tares? Why does a just and righteous God apparently exercise such callous disregard of our hard-fought moral and religious achievements?

Paul had an answer! "For God has consigned all (*all !*) to disobedience, *that he may have mercy upon all*" (Rom. 11:32, RSV, alt.). "Since all have sinned and fall short of the glory of God, they are justified by his grace as a gift, through the redemption that is in Christ Jesus" (Rom. 3:23–24, RSV). Martin Luther, with a deep grasp of the utterly subversive implications of all this, put the matter starkly: *If you want to be saved by Christ, you must first become a sinner!*

> Beware of aspiring to such purity that you will not wish to be looked upon as a sinner, or to be one. For Christ dwells only

in sinners. On this account he descended from heaven, where he dwelt among the righteous, to dwell among sinners. Meditate on this love of his and you will see his sweet consolation. For why was it necessary for him to die if we can obtain a good conscience by our works and afflictions? Accordingly you will find peace only in him and only when you despair of yourself and your own works. Besides, you will learn from him that just as he has received you, so he has made your sins his own and has made his righteousness yours.[2]

Jesus himself told us as much when he pointed out that those who are well have no need of a physician, but only those who are sick (Matt. 9:12). Paul in another place indicated that he himself, who had succeeded in keeping the law "blamelessly" (!), cast off his former achievement, considering it literally "dung," for the sake of being found in Christ Jesus (Phil. 3:4–10). The Lord who reigns from the cross is thus a Lord who surveys the whole wide landscape of human moral and religious striving and who in his own person bears it away into death, hell, and judgment.

Needless to say, this has profound effects on the shape of our life as a church, and it underscores the truth of Jesus' teaching that those who lose their life will find it. We become sinners as we come to Christ—we renounce and hand over every claim to moral and religious achievement and respectability. Along with such renunciation also comes a certain deliverance as well, however. Christ delivers us precisely from the self-deceiving exercises that are required to prop up our claims to righteousness, along with the constant comparisons to our more and less worthy neighbors that such a project inevitably entails. We renounce our works and our good deeds. We give up our claims to be or strive for anything apart from Christ. In place of all this we find simply . . . joy, thanksgiving, and freedom! Our obedience once given over is now handed back to us. It returns to us, not as our former, sometimes desperate striving, but as a new way of life that is given to us simply as spontaneous praise, as rejoicing in the Holy Spirit, free of any illusions as to its adequacy before God or its capacity to secure for us the kingdom. It is simply love. In Paul's image, we abound in thanksgiving (Col. 2:7), and this is enough, because in Christ we have been given all things. The Christian life is thus liberated from its grim and ultimately self-serving and self-deceiving seriousness and becomes instead "something beautiful for God," to use Mother Teresa's celebrated phrase.

This radically new existence of the believer in Christ transforms our relation with our neighbors, for it erases nearly all of the relevant distinctions between them and us. In the radiance of the cross of our crucified Lord, we see that *all* of us are sinners for whom Christ died. All of us are beggars before the throne of grace. All of us are the unworthy recipients of his gracious invitation to discipleship and eternal life. "God shows no partiality" (Rom. 2:11). It is no longer permissible or desirable to divide the spheres of our experience into those of the righteous church and the unrighteous world. We have in Christ renounced all calculation whether our neighbors are "worthy" of our kindness or God's grace. All such deliberations are crucified on the cross with Christ. Therefore we can be utterly profligate with our love of sinners, and our enfolding embrace of them into the transforming fellowship of Christ's body. Jesus Christ *is* God's mission to the world and—most especially!—*for* the world. To confess his Lordship is to be caught up ourselves into that mission, into that astonishing love of sinners, that shines forth so brightly from the cross. The crucified One is Lord!

The Lordship of the Risen and Exalted Son of God

> *Therefore God also highly exalted him and gave him the name that is above every name, so that at the name of Jesus every knee should bend, in heaven and on earth and under the earth, and every tongue should confess that Jesus Christ is Lord to the glory of God the Father.* (Phil. 2:9–11)

Christ is risen, triumphant, and coming again. He has defeated the powers of sin, death, and hell. His Lordship *will* be acknowledged—either triumphantly or despairingly—by every living creature. This being the case, let us consider briefly how acknowledgment of this all-encompassing dimension of Christ's Lordship affects our understanding of inclusiveness within the church.

Inclusiveness has come to be an extremely important concept within the life of the mainline Protestant churches. Within the PC(USA) it has been elevated to constitutional status, figuring prominently in the *Book of Order* as one of the guiding principles of church life.

Questions have swirled around this concept in recent times, with many persons arguing that the church's commitment here is incompatible with the enforcement of boundaries of various sorts within the life of the church. Within the Presbyterian Church (U.S.A.) in particular, many contend that the church constitution is divided against itself by its commitment to inclusiveness on the one hand and its stipulation of traditional standards of sexual morality as a qualification for ordination on the other.

Clearly the concept of inclusiveness requires clarification: for if it is taken as all-embracing, it leads into absurdity. What is there in principle to prevent, for instance, a fellowship of neo-Nazis demanding full acceptance on this basis into the life of the church? Such problems crop up when inclusiveness as a concept becomes dislodged from its scriptural moorings and as a free-floating abstraction begins to exercise a lordship of its own, independent of Christ's Lordship. The solution to the problem is neither to embrace the contradictions thus generated nor to dismiss the concept altogether, but to reestablish its anchor in the Lordship of Jesus Christ.

Inclusiveness is indeed a biblical concept. Though not identified by name in the biblical text, it certainly figures as a prominent and frequently scandalous feature of Jesus' ministry. Jesus' willingness to associate himself with lepers, prostitutes, tax collectors, outcasts, and sinners of every sort is a constant and shocking source of wonder and public dismay throughout the course of his ministry.

On the other hand, Jesus also displays a willingness to offend and alienate well-meaning people in a way that often strikes us as appalling. The rich young ruler he sends away sorrowful

(Mark 10:17ff.). Jesus teaches the crowds in parables in order to prevent their understanding (Matt. 13:10ff.). He is offensively emphatic in his talk about eating flesh and drinking blood, alienating multitudes of would-be disciples (John 6:66ff.) He responds with an abrupt rebuff to an eminently respectful overture from a prominent member of the Sanhedrin (John 3:1ff.). Jesus counsels his disciples to enter "by the narrow gate," accompanied by the grim warning that those who find it will be few (Matt. 7:13–14). Little of this seems to fit with the other, radically "inclusive" aspects of his ministry that we observe.

The clue to the puzzle is found in our confession of Christ as the Lord who is risen and coming again in glory to judge both the living and the dead. Every knee *will* bow to him and every tongue *will* confess him—not just Christian knees or tongues! In other words, *the ultimate destiny of every human being will be established and determined by his or her relationship to Jesus Christ*. This is the radically inclusive character of the gospel. There is not a man or woman who has ever lived who shall escape having to do, in an ultimate and determinative sense, with Jesus Christ. "I am the first and the last, and the living one; I died, and behold I am alive for evermore, and I have the keys of Death and Hades" (Rev. 1:17–18, RSV). Jesus' ministry, and the church's participation in that ministry by its engrafting into him, reflects this radically inclusive character of his Lordship. No human being stands outside the orbit of Christ's coming universal reign. The gospel message is decisively and critically relevant for every person in every place and every condition of life. It is inclusive in the fullest sense. For this reason there can never be *any* boundaries or restrictions on whom the church is willing to call and invite into the circle of Christ's disciples. The Lordship of Christ, and hence the saving relevance of the gospel, is universal and all-inclusive.

At the same time, Jesus' all-inclusive Lordship has to it a particular shape and character, for it represents the final triumph of the love of God, both for and among creatures. The kingdom over which Christ rules involves the final perfection of creatures in joyous communion with God and with one another, that God may be all in all. Christ's Lordship thus has a positive and very specific *content*, to which human lives may be conformed by faith, repentance, and sanctification. Lives that are *not* being conformed by grace to the shape of Christ's sovereign rule, lives that are on the contrary slowly hardening on foundations incompatible with the purified love of God and neighbor, are clearly in great jeopardy. The danger is not that persons leading such lives will never see or recognize the triumphant establishment of Christ's universal Lordship throughout every corner of the cosmos. *Every* knee shall bow! The danger is that by the time Christ ushers in the kingdom in its fullness, they will have become souls so misshapen and distorted by the ravages of sin that they will be unable to greet Christ's triumphant reign as anything other than catastrophe. Christ's reign will be their own contradiction, judgment, and disaster. For them Christ's Lordship will mean only the searing, all-encompassing awareness of the grace that they finally and irrevocably rejected.

For this reason the universal and all-inclusive *invitation* of the gospel is an invitation precisely to the discipleship of the narrow way. It is an invitation joyously to embrace the universal Lordship of Christ in faith, repentance, and a glorious new life in union with him. The inclusiveness of the gospel is not an inclusiveness that encompasses many kinds of discipleship and thus many different lords. It is an inclusiveness that *universally* proclaims the *one* Lord Jesus Christ, joyously and humbly, and that offers the loving and faithful fellowship of the *one* universal communion of Christ's church, to every wandering child of God, without reservation or scruple or exception. The Lord is risen. Even so, come, Lord Jesus!

NOTES

1. See the discussion at the end of book II, chapter 3, "The Shocking Alternative," in C. S. Lewis, *Mere Christianity* (New York: Macmillan Co., 1943).
2. Martin Luther, "Letter to George Spenlein, April 8, 1516," WA, Br 1, 33–36; quoted in John W. Doberstein, *A Minister's Prayer Book* (Philadelphia: Muhlenberg Press, 1960), 230–31.

Two-Handed Holiness

1 Peter 1:13–16

M. Craig Barnes

M ost of us yearn to do that which is right and good and holy, but we cannot always find the way. We don't mean to lie, or cheat, or disobey God. We just find it to be an unfortunate necessity sometimes. After all, we live in a fallen world. Things get complicated down here, and often you have to bend a rule or two. You have to do the wrong thing to get to the right place. You can't be too high and mighty about your principles. We know it's wrong to sacrifice our principles, but we tell ourselves we really have no choice. We echo the words of the small child who, when the teacher asked, "What is a lie?" responded by saying, "A lie is an abomination to God, and a very present help in times of trouble."

It would be nice to be holy. But most of us think that is no longer possible for us. Things have gone too far. We have made too many compromises with the truth. We have grown accustomed to our besetting sins and weaknesses, and to living in a world that knows little of true holiness.

As much as we may try to settle for this profane existence, though, we never can. That's because we have these souls that are so homesick for heaven they long to find a glimpse of something that is truly holy. Not finding this in ourselves, we begin to search for it in other places. But we cannot find anything that inspires us with awe and wonder, fear and reverence.

So when Peter quotes God, saying, "You shall be holy, for I am holy" (1 Peter 1:16, RSV), it is easy to start despairing. How are we going to do that? With more oughts and shoulds and religious prescriptions? We've tried that. We're still trying that. And no matter how hard we try, we can't seem to be good enough. In fact, the harder we try, the more mistakes we make. When we come to the silent confession in worship, who among us find they have nothing to say? If you're like me, you have so much to say that you run out of time.

But maybe it is appropriate that the pastor interrupts our confession with the marvelous declaration, "In Jesus Christ we are forgiven." Or as Peter writes, "Set all your hope on the grace that Jesus Christ will bring you" (1 Peter 1:13, NRSV). Now that does not simply mean that Jesus forgives our sins from last week so we can start over this week with a futile effort to be holy. Rather, it means that in Jesus Christ we receive a holiness we will never attain on our own. As Calvin frequently reminded us in the *Institutes*,[1] every part of our salvation is already complete in Christ by virtue of his obedience for us, and the Spirit's invitation to live our life in Christ.

So when Peter quotes the Lord saying, "You shall be holy, for I am holy," he is not giving us an imperative. He is making a promise! In Jesus Christ, you *shall* be holy. We don't become holy by trying to follow Jesus' teachings. Rather, we are made holy by drawing so close to Jesus that his love begins to flow through our veins, changing our hearts, renewing our minds, and making us holy in every aspect of life.

In order to understand the New Testament teaching on this, we first have to return in the Old Testament to Leviticus, where this marvelous phrase about being holy first appears. The Levitical law called the Hebrews to be holy in every aspect of their lives. Their relationships with family, with the community, and the king were all to be holy. They had holy days, holy clothes, holy utensils, holy washings, holy sacrifices, holy food, and the list goes on and on. None of these things were holy in themselves, but all of them were made holy as they were used to draw people to the Lord Jehovah who was in their midst. The dwelling place of Jehovah was in a sacred room called the Holy of Holies, which was in the center of the Tabernacle and the Temple, which in turn was in the center of their community. All of life was made holy by its center in the Holy of Holies, where holiness resided.

But in Jesus Christ, God took on flesh and dwelt among us. This created a new means for becoming holy, as we now found our center in him. Remember how confusing it was when Jesus kept explaining that the Temple would be destroyed and in three days it would rise again? He was making the incredible claim that he was the new dwelling place of God's holiness. Remember how the veil that separated the Holy of Holies from the world was ripped from top to bottom at Jesus' death on the cross? When God did that, he made his holiness accessible to the whole world. It could now make its way into every corner and crevice of the world, wherever the risen Jesus took it. Expounding upon the significance of this, Paul claimed that for those who are in Christ, all food is clean, all days are holy, all places are sacred. All work done in the name of Jesus is now the work of priests. In Christ there is no distinction between secular and sacred. It's all sacred because he is in our midst.

This means that your days, which are packed with car pools, dirty laundry, copy machines that jam when you need them most, phones that keep ringing, committee meetings that go on so long you start to believe in the doctrine of purgatory, are all within the realm of holiness. All of it can be an opportunity to encounter the sacred for which our souls yearn, if you can look for Jesus who is there.

One of the earliest heresies that the church had to struggle with was Gnosticism, which is still alive and well in the church today. The Gnostics wanted badly to ascend to holiness and decided that the problem was with this fallen, sinful world. If they were ever going to become holy, they were going to have to just nurture the life of the spirit and ignore the concerns of this life.

When the early church father Irenaeus challenged this heresy, he wrote about the two hands of God. One of those hands is Jesus Christ, the Word of God made flesh, who descends into our midst and makes life holy by his presence. The other hand is the Spirit of God, who lifts us up and engrafts us into the risen Christ. God the Father uses both of those hands, Irenaeus said, to embrace us. That is ministry of the blessed Trinity. Like the prodigal son's father, who wraps both hands around him, embracing him, kissing him, rejoicing that the lost is found, so does God take us in both arms. This isn't some wimpy, one-arm, side embrace. The Son and the Spirit become God's two-handed embrace that draws all of life into his holiness.

Salvation means that when God finds us he receives everything. He rejects nothing. Certainly not our ordinary routines. But not even our great regrets. When we give to God the great mistakes and sins of our past, we discover there is a holy use for everything. In God's hands life is no longer a challenge to get right. It is a holy gift to be received with awe and reverence and humble faithfulness. Even the simplest and most ordinary work, if done to the glory of God, can become an opportunity to hear the seraphim singing, "Holy, holy, holy is the LORD of hosts; The whole earth is full of his glory" (Isa. 6:3, NRSV).

NOTE

1. Calvin, *Institutes of the Christian Religion* II.xvi.17.

The Punch Line of the Gospel

Philippians 1:27–2:12

Theresa Ip Froehlich

Presbyterian pastor Roger and his family were taking their vacation in the Pocono Mountains. On a lazy Sunday, they worshiped at a little Methodist church. It was a hot day. The heat and the sultry air were making people drowsy. The preacher was preaching up a storm while the folks in the pews were struggling to keep their eyes open until all of a sudden he said, "The best years of my life have been spent in the arms of another man's wife."

The whole congregation gasped and came to immediate attention. The dozing deacon in the back row dropped his hymnbook, and the usher next to him sheepishly looked around to see if anybody had noticed he was dozing. The whole sanctuary was in such still and silent suspense one could hear a pin drop.

Then the preacher added, "It was my mother."

The congregation giggled a little and managed to stay awake till the end of the sermon. Pastor Roger registered the experience in his memory, since it was such a good trick to regain the congregation's attention.

On a hot lazy Sunday the following summer, Pastor Roger was preaching in his home church. The flies were buzzing around, and the ushers were sinking lower and lower in the back row. Then he remembered the trick he learned at the Methodist church in the Pocono Mountains, so he said in a loud, booming voice, "The best years of my life have been spent in the arms of another man's wife." Pastor Roger got their attention. One of the ushers in the back row sat up so fast he hit his head on the back of the pew in front of him. Roger had them in the palm of his hands. But he forgot what came next. All he could think to say was, "And for the life of me, I can't remember her name!"

Pastor Roger got himself into trouble because he forgot the punch line of his joke. Instead of regaining the congregation's attention to hear his message, he led them to believe something that was not true.

A few years ago, George Barna did a study on the biblical knowledge of churchgoing Christians and discovered that the majority of them cannot articulate the gospel. The apostle Paul recognizes how critical it is to remember the punch line of the gospel: Jesus Christ is Lord (Phil. 2:11). In a variety of places in his letters, Paul puts the gospel in capsule form: "that Christ died for our sins according to the Scriptures, that he was buried, that he was raised on the third day according to the Scriptures" (1 Cor. 15:3, NIV). He also lists God's expectation for the gospel community: "Whatever happens, conduct yourselves in a manner worthy of the gospel of Christ" (Phil. 1:27).

Paul's summary of the gospel of Jesus Christ teaches three key elements in our relationship with God: our *transgression* against the holy God, God the Son's *transaction* to pay for our sin, and our *transformation* by God the Holy Spirit. These three key elements are like the legs of a three-legged stool, which cannot stand if one of its legs is missing.

Our *transgression* against the holy God is the bad news about us. The bad news is the condition of sin in our human nature that causes us to be hostile to God, to hold attitudes displeasing to God, and to behave in ways annoying to God so that we are the objects of his wrath (Rom. 1:18; Eph. 2:3). Paul found himself commanding the Christian community in Philippi to live out their citizenship of God's kingdom because they were not already doing so. The Philippian believers were still living in transgression.

There is more bad news about us. Being "without hope and without God in the world" (Rom. 1:18–32; 3:9–20; Eph. 2:1–3, 12), we are not only caught in the hopeless condition of sin, but we are also helpless and unable to save ourselves. In spite of our animosity towards God, he took the initiative to reconcile us to himself through the vicarious death of his own Son, Jesus Christ (Eph. 2:4–10; Rom. 3:21–24). This sacrificial death of God the Son is the historical *transaction* that made him our one and only way to salvation, our one and only way to God (John 14:6; John 10:7–9; Acts 4:12).

The moment we place our personal trust in Jesus Christ, we have completed a transaction with Christ to acknowledge him Lord and Savior by entering into union with him—as born-again children of God (John 1:12) and as a new creation (2 Cor. 5:17). This moment marks the beginning of the *transformation* process as the Holy Spirit conforms us to God's image. Genuine faith in Jesus Christ shows itself in growing dependence on him as Lord and growing obedience to the divine commands, though this obedience is not the grounds on which God declares us righteous.

The gospel then is really the good news announcing to the world that "change" for the better is not only possible but also real. God the Son said yes to the Father when he gave his own life on the cross. In response to the Son's obedient act, God the Father said yes to the Son by making him Lord of all (Phil. 2:8–11). We as God's people are daily to say yes to the Lord Jesus Christ as the Holy Spirit works to change us. The Lordship of Jesus Christ is thus significant in three ways for those of us who claim to be followers of Jesus Christ.

First, the gospel of Jesus Christ is not primarily about me or about humankind; it is not about the improvement of the human condition. It is primarily about God, who in his saving grace initiated his plan of salvation and who through his sanctifying grace changes us from the inside out so that we may conform to his standards.

Second, Christ's self-sacrifice bought our freedom from the power of sin, but it did not give us the freedom to sin. God's law remains effective: it is not those who slavishly and outwardly observe the law who are righteous in God's eyes but those who joyfully obey the law due to an inner change of heart (Rom. 2:13; cf. 3:20).

Third, the gospel community is God's work-in-progress. We are a people in the process of becoming, and so we live with the tension of "already but not yet." We are sojourners on the journey to perfection, yet we stumble along the way. We are a forgiven people, yet we continually need God's forgiveness. We are a transformed people, yet we are still in the process of being transformed. This is why Paul assures us that "he who began a good work in [us] will carry it on to completion until the day of Christ Jesus" (Phil. 1:6, NIV). This is also why Paul urges us to "continue to work out [our] salvation with fear and trembling" (Phil. 2:12, NIV).

In a nutshell, Jesus Christ changes individual lives as each of his followers, having been united with him ("in Christ," Phil. 2:1), obeys him as he obeyed his Father. The Lordship of Jesus Christ compels us to match our words with our works so that we do not become theological schizophrenics. It keeps us from being guilty of hypocrisy—the hypocrisy of professing to be followers of Christ but not living under his Lordship.

The Philippian Christians were guilty of this hypocrisy because some were showing behaviors motivated by "selfish ambition" and "vain conceit" (Phil. 2:3). Paul's challenge to the Philippian Christians and to us is this: Don't just talk the talk, but also walk the walk. The career of following Jesus Christ requires not only confessing him as Savior but also obeying him as Lord, so that the church of Jesus Christ does not become an organization of schizophrenics and hypocrites.

As we try to walk the walk each day, we flesh out the practical implications of Christ's Lordship. The Lordship of Jesus Christ means at least three things: first, Jesus Christ claims exclusive loyalty from those who profess faith in him; second, he charges his followers to live obedient lives; third, he creates genuine community by changing individuals.

Refusing to grasp his status as God, Jesus humbled himself to break into human history as a person of no power, status, or significance and died the most horrifying death as a defenseless criminal. This act of self-sacrifice earned Jesus Christ, and no one else, the "Lordship." Jesus Christ, and none other, has earned the exclusive claim to our personal loyalty. Writing from the prison in Rome, Paul was well aware of Emperor Nero's lust for absolute power and his demand to be called "lord." Against this background of competing lords and saviors, Paul risked his personal safety to proclaim that there is no Lord under heaven except Jesus Christ, that there is no legitimate CEO on earth except Jesus Christ.

In our time, these competing lords are often not personal but philosophical or ideological. They frequently take the form of worldviews, philosophies, or pathways to salvation. Many of these are even cloaked in Christian vocabulary. These competing worldviews and philosophies ultimately deny that Jesus Christ is Lord. About four years ago at Montreat, North Carolina, I attended a theological conference with about a hundred Presbyterian pastors and lay leaders. One morning at breakfast table I struck up a conversation with an elder who had been in the Presbyterian Church all his life. He believed that Jesus Christ was his savior, but he also believed that all religions take us to heaven because they all teach human beings to do good.

A story illustrates this syncretistic mindset of our time. Father O'Casey, the parish priest, was administering the last rites to a critically ill parishioner, Billy Flaherty. Before anointing Billy with oil, Father O'Casey asked, "Do you renounce the world, the flesh, and the devil?" Billy replied, "I think in my condition this is no time to offend anyone."

Jesus Christ is not impressed that people believe in him and take him as one savior among many savior candidates. By the same token, God was not impressed with the people of Israel who believed in him and at the same time worshiped Baal and followed the pagan practices. The key problem with God's people in the Old Testament time was not atheism (the belief in no God) but syncretism (a kind of salad-bar religion that embraces the one true God and other false gods all at the same time). In contrast to this syncretism, the Committee on Evangelical Unity in the Gospel has recently issued a statement called "The Gospel of Jesus Christ: An Evangelical Celebration," which clearly affirms that "the biblical doctrine of justification by faith alone in Christ alone is essential to the Gospel."[1]

Jesus Christ is not interested in job-sharing with other competing lords and saviors. He wants monopoly rights to our personal loyalty, and nothing less. As he exercises his monopoly rights, he charges professing Christians to live obedient lives in the same pattern as his own obedience. In order to live out our citizenship in a manner worthy of the gospel, we are to: (1) perform responsibilities as citizens of our heavenly homeland (Phil. 1:27a), instead of demanding rights and privileges; (2) protect the witness of the gospel by advancing it with holy, obedient living (Phil. 1:27b), instead of damaging it with unholy lifestyles; (3) prefer the concerns and needs of others over our own (Phil. 2:3–4), because self-giving is God's character trait.

Fulfilling this charge requires a new life-orientation that is not absorbed with the self but is instead centered on and obedient to Jesus Christ as Lord. A Christ-centered and obedient community is effective for the advance of the gospel, a key concern for Paul in his letter to the Philippians (Phil. 1:12). The progress of the gospel works like wagon wheels. When the spokes are properly hooked up to the hub at the center, the wheels can rotate and take the wagon to its destination. However, if the spokes are hooked up to something other than Christ the center, the gospel wagon will not go anywhere.

Finally, Jesus Christ creates genuine community by changing the individuals in the gospel community into his likeness. The community grows in visible unity as each one is being transformed into a Christlike character by the power of the Holy Spirit. To become part of the gospel community, a person must first be initiated into the community by being united with Christ. Christ's community is not primarily a liturgical community bound together by the rites; rather it is a saved and surrendered community bound together by our union in Christ and the Lordship of Christ. As a result, unity among the followers of

Jesus Christ cannot be attained by religion, sacraments, or institutional membership; it can be attained only by a genuine and growing relationship with and in the Lord Jesus Christ.

A genuine and growing relationship with Jesus Christ is evidenced by our commitment to imitate Christ. As the Holy Spirit empowers us to deny our "selves," we say no to a culture that constantly urges us to serve and gratify our "selves" and to demand rights and privileges. This then allows the progress of the gospel (Phil. 2:2) to emerge as the top priority for the faith community. This united purpose is what brings unity to the community.

As the faith community grows in Christlike character, it becomes an effective community that can influence the world. It becomes a quality mirror that accurately reflects the image of Jesus Christ to the world. It is only as a people of God together that God's people can fulfil his divine purposes.

In a time when the church of Jesus Christ confronts a less-than-friendly culture, the faith community can be an effective instrument in God's hands only if we live out our citizenship of God's kingdom. We do this, not only by talking the talk as we proclaim Jesus Christ as Savior, but by walking the walk as we obey Jesus Christ as Lord.

The church of Jesus Christ is charged with the Great Commission to "go and make disciples . . ., baptizing them . . . and teaching them to obey . . ." (Matt. 28:19–20, NIV). God's people can be effective in fulfilling this charge only if we know for whom we are making disciples, in whose name we are baptizing, and what we are expected to teach. It is time to reclaim our responsibility to teach the gospel to the next generation with the same urgency and intensity that Paul had: "For what I received I passed on to you as of first importance" (1 Cor. 15:3, NIV). The diligent "passing on" from one generation to the next is the way to ensure that we do not forget the punch line of the gospel: Jesus Christ is Lord.

NOTE

1. *Christianity Today*, June 14, 1999, 51.

PART 2

Union with Christ
through Word
and Sacrament

God's Speech and Our Preaching

Elizabeth Achtemeier

In the story of the garden of Eden, in the third chapter of Genesis, the "subtle" serpent entices Eve to step outside of her intimate relation with the God who has created her and to talk about God as an object. Unfortunately, that is the picture of God presupposed by many contemporary sermons, and it certainly is the conception of God that many modern worshipers have. God is an object—an object out there, to be discussed. We can decide who he is and how he is to be imagined. We can judge whether or not he is trustworthy and whether or not we can believe in him. We can accept him or reject him as we will, and practically, many think that it does not make a great deal of difference. God is an object.

Sermons that deal with such an object God therefore may urge us to seek the Lord and to find him. They may admonish us to praise him and to pray to him. They often tell us to repent and mend our ways, and thus be relieved of our burden of guilt. Then we can know that we are loved and accepted no matter what we have done. To be sure, such sermons may describe the characteristics of this object God at great length in various propositions: "God is love." "He is everywhere." "God is like a mother." But the telling point is that we worshipers remain the actors

43

toward God. He doesn't do much of anything. He is just there. Ours is the action, and our attitude, our faith, and our commitment determine what the relation between the Lord and us will be. We act. God receives.

A genuine biblical understanding of preaching turns such relations upside down. If we study the scriptures carefully, it becomes clear that the primary actor in the divine-human relationship is God. Throughout the writings of the Bible, the initial action is always God's. Human beings, then, are required to respond. The scriptures never reveal God as an object to be found. Indeed, it is impossible for us human beings to find God. Can men and women search out God? asks the book of Job, and the answer is No (Job 11:7; 23:3; 37:23). Rather, the command is, "Seek the LORD *while he may be found,* call upon him *while he is near*" (Isa. 55:6, RSV), that is, while the Lord has drawn near to receive us. Unless God reveals himself to us, we cannot know him. The first move is always God's move. His must always be the initial approach to us and the initial revelation of himself. It is only as the Lord reveals himself that we are asked to respond to that disclosure. The revelatory history preserved for us in the scriptures is one long dialogue or story in which God acts and speaks in a multitude of ways, making known his will and character. Individuals, societies, and nations are then portrayed in their equally multitudinous responses to that divine action. God speaks and acts, humans respond. God acts and speaks accordingly further, and the dialogical story goes on and on. It has to be told largely in story form, because only stories recount what has taken place.

Implications for Preaching

Certainly the ultimate intention of Christian preaching is to lead the congregation into a relationship with the triune God in Jesus Christ. To be sure, some sermons may have only a teaching function, to instruct and educate the congregation in the basic doctrines and ethics of the Christian faith. The Christian ignorance of most average churchgoers pleads for more educational sermons. Finally, however, doctrine is worthless and ethics are hollow unless they are grounded in a living relationship with God, as Isaiah points out (Isa. 29:13–14).

Genuine biblical preaching is preaching through which the triune God acts and speaks to reveal himself to his gathered people. Only if God's is the initial action, drawing near to his people and revealing himself through the words of the sermon, can the congregation possibly know God and enter into relationship with him. In short, biblical preaching is sacramental preaching, that is, it is preaching that depends and relies upon God's acts toward us. Sacrifices are actions in which we act toward God. But sacraments are actions in which God acts toward us, and biblical preaching is intended to mediate that divine action.

Biblical preaching is thus not designed just to influence human actions, thoughts, and feelings, though certainly it hopes such influence will result. It is not moralistic exhortation or manipulative inspiration, using clever and moving illustrations. It is not intended as a presentation of the pastor's views or of some faddish subject of the day. Above all, it is not a performance on the pastor's part or simply entertainment for the audience. No. Genuine biblical preaching is an avenue, along with the sacraments, of God's speaking and acting toward us. Through the human words of the sermon, we pray and hope and trust that God will speak to his people and do his deeds in their lives.

The triune God may do all sorts of things through the sermon. He may call our whole lifestyle into question and prompt us to examine ourselves and to repent. He may strengthen us in a faith we already have or deepen our understanding of his relation with us. He may comfort us in some sorrow or still our anxiety over a troubling situation we face. He often takes the burden of our guilt from us and assures us of his forgiveness through Jesus Christ. Frequently, he instills in us the certain hope of eternal life, and often he causes us to want to praise him. Sometimes he just overawes us with his glorious presence. Whatever the action the Lord chooses to work toward us in any given worship service, we find ourselves the recipients of the words and deeds of the Lord himself when a sermon is preached according to the scriptures.

The Work of the Bible

Obviously, such a sacramental understanding of preaching necessitates that the scriptural text or texts chosen for the day form the basis of the sermon. Through no other medium has the Lord God fully revealed himself except through the witness of Israel in the Old Testament and the testimonies about Jesus Christ and the early church in the New Testament. The heavens may tell the glory of God, according to Psalm 19, but it is finally the Word of the Lord that revives, makes wise, rejoices, and enlightens, sings that psalmist. If we seek to know God only through nature, we end up with a world "red of tooth and claw," and we have finally to realize that in the struggle of fallen nature, the big gods just eat the little gods.

If we look for God in the depths of ourselves, "Selfishness" becomes his name, and we have to admit that there is no pure truth or goodness in the divinity we ascribe to ourselves. If the arts, the beauty of music, the forms of sculpture and painting, or the vitality of dance are our source of revelation, then they crumble and fade, tire and pass away, while the God of the scriptures is the everlasting Father, who is before and after all human construction. It has pleased God to speak and act toward us through the sacred history of his people Israel, and supremely through the life, death, and resurrection of his Son, Jesus Christ, as those are illumined for us and brought home to our hearts and minds through the action of the Holy Spirit. While many other forms of communication—the words of an anthem, the portrayal in a stained-glass window, the words of a Christian friend—may convey the biblical stories to us, all of those extrabiblical forms take their validity from the scriptures and reveal God truly only as they accord with the witness of the scripture. In the Bible we have the canon, the measuring rod, of the triune God's true speech and action.

It follows therefore that preaching, in order to mediate God's speaking and action to the listening congregation, must find its source in the Bible. Some preachers take their texts from poems or hymns, or even from the morning headlines. But they have thereby abandoned any authoritative base for their sermons. Who cares, finally, what human opinions they bring forth? Human views have no authority. All authority has been given to Jesus Christ (Matt. 28:18). And it is, indeed, our Lord Jesus Christ who is finally the center and subject of the scriptures. The Old Testament looks forward to him, the New Testament remembers him. And when he is portrayed in his incarnation in human flesh, his Person gathers up the whole witness of the Old Testament and brings it to its final fulfillment and reinterpretation. Christ becomes, in fact, the whole Word of God made flesh (John 1). The triune God who speaks and acts toward us through the scriptures is the Son of the Father, revealed to us by the Holy Spirit, and it is supremely our Lord Christ who approaches us and enters into relationship with us through the words of a biblical sermon. To preach a Christian sermon is to follow the practice of Paul, "I decided to know nothing among you except Jesus Christ and him crucified"—"the power of God and the wisdom of God." Christ is our "wisdom, our righteousness and sanctification and redemption," writes Paul (1 Cor. 2:2; 1:24, 30, RSV). Therefore Christian sermons aim toward our union with Christ, in whom we are given our salvation.

That does not mean that every sermon must finally end with the cross and resurrection. The Old Testament bears within itself the preparatory revelations for Christ's coming, and there are multitudes among us who need that preparation. Indeed, it is impossible to know who Jesus Christ is apart from the Old Testament, for our Lord is described in the New Testament almost totally in the terms of the Old Testament's theologies. Equally, it is impossible to know who we are as the church, unless we find our beginnings and root in the covenant people of Israel. We Gentiles are the "wild branches" grafted into the root of Israel (Rom. 11:17–24), and thereby made members of Israel's unique status and calling—God's "chosen race," "royal priesthood," "holy nation" (1 Peter 2:9; Ex. 19:5–6), given the task, like God's witness Israel, to "declare the wonderful deeds of him who called [us] out of darkness into his marvelous light" (1 Peter 2:9, RSV). Separated from the commonwealth of Israel, we were "no people" (1 Peter 2:10), "without God in the world" (Eph. 2:12). Grafted into the "covenants of promise," we have become "God's people." It is necessary in Christian preaching that we hear such things and know who we are in God's world.

Indeed, it is folly for Christian preachers and laity to ignore that confession of faith that we call the Old Testament, because our own story as God's covenant people is writ large on the pages of the book of the Old Covenant. Both Israel and we were delivered from slavery, long before we had worked any piety or done anything to deserve our redemption—Israel from her bondage in Egypt, we from our slavery to sin and death. Both Israel and we have been accompanied every step along the way through our wilderness journeys of life by the Lord who promised, "I am with you always." Both of us are brought to the table of covenant, Israel on Sinai and in its Passover, we at the Lord's Supper. There we eat and drink with our Lord, and there we promise to serve and obey the one true God alone. Both of us are given commandments in God's love to guide our paths on the way to abundant life, being asked to love the Lord our God with all our heart and mind and strength, and our neighbor as ourselves. Both of us are God's witnesses to the world of his forgiving and saving love. Both of us bring our sacrifices of praise and thanksgiving to worship him. Both of us travel toward the promised place of rest—Israel toward the promised land and Jerusalem, we toward the new Jerusalem in the kingdom of God. Israel's story is the story of our journey with God, and no Christian preacher should ignore that twelve hundred years of Israel's experience with the Lord that can serve as the analogy and guide for our experience with him also. Thus, Christian sermons should take their texts from the Old Testament as well as the New and fully proclaim them.

One qualification is in order. When the Old Testament is the source of the principal text for a sermon, it should always be paired with a New Testament text, for finally we have to ask what happened to God's words to Israel. The Old Testament ends in promise, up in the air, with no fulfillment given, and we finally have to point out the completion in, or at least the preparation for, Jesus Christ. Sometimes preachers will preach only from an Old Testament text and then, toward the end of the sermon, drag in a general reference to Christ in order to make the sermon Christian. But the good news of the gospel is not given to us in general; it is given in the very specific deeds and words of God preserved for us in the New Testament. And we must preach that specificity. God's words and acts are tied to real history, not to pious generalities.

It is the unique character of the scriptures that they not only tell us what God has said and done in the past, but by the action of the Holy Spirit, those deeds and acts are made actual for us in the present. For example, when we read the story of Jesus' last supper with his disciples, that does not remain just an interesting narrative about the past. Rather, through the story, we are there, eating and drinking with our Lord and hearing that one of us will betray him. We are there, like the disciples certain of our loyalty and exclaiming in dismay, "Lord, surely not I!" "Were you there when they crucified my Lord?" Yes, indeed, we were and are. And "sometimes it causes me to tremble." The Holy Spirit makes the scripture from the past our present reality; it takes us into its narrative and makes us recipients of its action. Jesus gasps from the cross, "Father, forgive them for they know not what they do." And you and I in the congregation of worshipers find ourselves in fact forgiven.

This work of the scriptures, by which they make their past our present, was well known already to Israel, and so in their liturgies they recited the stories of what God had done for them in the past. Similarly, we tell what happened "on the night when he was betrayed" when we celebrate anew the Lord's Supper. By that recitation, God's acts toward the Israel of the past became the deeds that he is doing toward his people in the present.

For example, at the ceremony of the presentation of the first-fruits to God in the temple, the worshiping Israelite recited Israel's history. "A wandering Aramean was my father; and he went down into Egypt and sojourned there, few in number; and there he became a nation, mighty, and populous" (Deut. 26:5, RSV)—that's all in the past. But then, in the recital of faith, the pronouns change: "And the Egyptians treated *us* harshly, and afflicted *us* . . . and the LORD heard *our* voice, and saw *our* afflic- tion . . . and the LORD brought *us* out of Egypt, with a mighty hand and an outstretched arm" (vv. 6–8). Thus, the redemption of Israel from Egyptian slavery is no longer an event that God worked only in the past, but, through the use of the sacred story, it becomes a redemption from bondage worked in the present for the confessing worshiper. The work, the action of the scrip- ture, by the mercy of God, turns past divine action into the pre- sent work of the Lord.

Certainly we want our congregations to experience in their lives the redemption, the correction and judgment, the forgive- ness and justification, the transforming sanctification and growth in the Spirit that belong to the Christian life. In short, we want them to experience Christ and be united with him, because in him alone is the way to the Father and the truth of God and the abundant life that comes from him. But if we want that for our people, then there is only one way to provide it—by preaching the scriptures, whose subject is Jesus Christ.

The Approach to the Bible

It is significant that we do not preach *about* the scriptures. We preach the scriptures. It is always tempting for homileticians to turn a text into an object—to stand back from the passage and to discuss it, to decide what is true about it or what is not, to cri- tique it from the standpoint of history or sociology, archaeology or psychology. (Preachers sometimes think to prompt a lot of admiration for their scholarly learning.) And to be sure, often a text must be set in its historical context or have some explanation given of its terms and variety of meanings. But that necessity is quite subsidiary to the primary content of the sermon, for if the text is objectified throughout the sermon, the preacher has placed him or herself between the congregation and the speak- ing of God through the text. There is a great difference between saying, "The Bible says, 'Your sins are forgiven,' " and the procla- mation, "Your sins are forgiven." In the former, the preacher speaks; in the latter, God himself. God in Christ, when he so wills, by the illumination of the Holy Spirit, addresses his gathered people through the instrument of the sermon, and the preacher is simply the meeting point between that divine address and the congregation. The best role of the preacher, therefore, is simply to take himself or herself out of the way and let the Lord speak and work.

For this reason, the primary style of preaching should be direct address. The Lord is speaking to his people, and that directness should be mirrored in the preacher's words. The prophets knew that secret. Through their words, God addressed Israel directly. "Thus says the Lord," began the prophets, and then they proclaimed God's words, in which the Lord himself confronted his people and demanded of them a response.

That style óf preaching is fostered by all sorts of means that are found in the scriptures themselves—by questions: "Is it not so?"; by imperatives: "Behold!"; by personal pronouns: "You and I"; by descriptions: "We do," "we are," "we think." The point is that the scriptures mediate God speaking directly to us, and the sermon should strive to preserve that directness. "Never let them go!" is the watchword for the preacher. That is, the congregation must know that the sermon is directed to them.

In approaching a text, we must also keep in mind that God speaks through the Old Testament as well as through the New. The common stereotype applied to the Old Testament is that it is full of God's judgment toward Israel, which is then overcome in the gracious words and deeds of the Lord Christ. But as we have pointed out, the Christian church is the "Israel of God" also, according to Paul (Gal. 6:16). Therefore, we preachers should be very hesitant to dismiss any of God's words to Israel as inapplicable to us and our congregation. For example, in Amos 3:2 (RSV), the Lord declares, "You only have I known of all the families of the earth; therefore I will punish you for all your iniquities." That is God addressing not only the Israel of the eighth century B.C. It is also God addressing us as the new Israel in Jesus Christ, and so we must ask, "How is God working out that punishment of our iniquities, of us who are also his chosen people?" Or to give another example, in Hosea 2:14–20, the Lord promises whoring Israel that he will begin his sacred history with her all over again, leading her once more into the wilderness, speaking tenderly to her heart, and transforming her character until she is righteous and faithful toward him, her divine husband. How is it, then, that the Lord fulfills that promise? Where does he begin a new sacred history with his people? The original Israel to whom Hosea speaks has vanished into history, swallowed up by the Assyrian Empire. Does God's word still stand, and is it being fulfilled for us? These ancient words of the Old Testament are also God's words to us. The realization of that fact can lead us to deeper understandings when we ask how they apply to us.

Getting inside the Scriptures

In studying the text that is to be the basis of the sermon, the preacher will certainly want to use all of the tools available for uncovering the meaning of a biblical passage—and that includes historical criticism. That particular biblical science has a bad name among many conservative preachers and laity, because it has been misused by some to judge the historical facticity of a text, with no thought given to its canonical standing. But historical criticism, when properly used, is ignored to our loss, because the words of the Bible and the deeds of God recounted in it are not some sort of "eternal truths" removed from history. No. God did actually speak his word at specific times and in specific places in the lives of human beings, and he did in fact do concrete deeds in actual human history. The Word did in truth become flesh! He was not divorced from time and space. And so the historical settings of God's actions and words in the Bible can be studied by historical methods. In relation to what human situation did God speak and act? That is important to know. For example, it makes a difference in our understanding of the text to know to whom chapters 40–55 or 56–66 in the book of Isaiah were first delivered.

Similarly, God's deeds and words are preserved for us in the scriptures in a multitude of literary forms—in sagas, letters, poetry, oracles, folk tales, parables, wisdom sayings, dialogues, etc. Knowing the literary form by means of literary criticism can therefore enlighten us as to how to understand a passage. Is some parable ever to be interpreted allegorically? The answer to that makes a difference.

To mention other branches of biblical study, it makes a difference to learn the sociological setting of any biblical passage, just as it makes a difference if we know the geography, customs, religious beliefs, worship patterns, anthropological views, or etymological background of the passage's words. The various branches of biblical scholarship have helped us to know all those things. The preacher can rely on a vast body of previous work to help uncover a text's background, setting, and original meaning.

What such scholarship cannot uncover for the preacher, however, is the speaking of God through the text. For that revelation, all science is inadequate. The illumination by the Holy Spirit alone suffices, and the preacher can only wait in prayer and faith and surrender for the Spirit's enlightenment. After he or she has checked out the critical facts in commentaries and biblical dictionaries, the preacher's principal job becomes that of listening to the text. Without that prayerful, committed listening and meditation on the text for the day, no worthy sermon can emerge.

How do you *listen* to a biblical passage? How do you get inside of it? Perhaps one of the most helpful approaches is that called rhetorical analysis.

Most of the Bible's words first were shaped in oral form before ever being committed to writing. And through the Bible's words, the Lord God Almighty is speaking. So one of the most helpful approaches is to uncover the patterns of the speech—its repetitions, exclamations, questions, parallelisms, contrasts, particles, beginnings and endings, and so forth. For example, Deut. 8:7–18 is a stated Old Testament text for Thanksgiving Day in the common lectionary. If we ask what is the primary thrust of that text, it becomes clear from the repetitions that "forgetting" (vv. 11, 14, 19) and "remembering"(v. 18) form the central

motif—"You shall remember the LORD your God" (v. 18, RSV).
And what is Thanksgiving but remembering our Lord and the
long way he has brought us and the great things he has done for
us? Through the words of Moses in the text, God is telling us,
"Remember!"

Or let us take as an example the Bible's use of the little particle "for" (*ki* in the Hebrew; *gar* in the Greek). It could be translated "because." Thus, in Psalm 98, as is true in most hymnic
forms, we read, "Sing to the LORD a new song," and then, "for
(because) he has done marvelous things" (v. 1). The sentence
that begins with the particle *ki* gives the reason for the praise.
And the reason given can then furnish the major content of a sermon that calls for the praise of God. Similarly, in Jesus' words in
Mark 8:34–38, our Lord teaches, "If any man would come after
me, let him deny himself and take up his cross and follow me" (v.
34, RSV). The four following verses, then, all begin with that little word "for" (*gar*), and each of them tells the reason why we
should let our old selves be crucified and follow Jesus. Surely
those four reasons suggest the content of the sermon on the passage! The use of such rhetorical analysis can be an enormous
help in allowing us to get inside the principal thrust of a text in
order to develop a sermon from it.

Another tool that allows us to enter into a biblical passage is
the well-known Reformed dictum, "The scriptures interpret the
scriptures." First, that means that we must always pay attention
to the context of a passage. For example, Luke 18:1–8, apart
from its context, is sometimes interpreted allegorically as a call
to constant prayer. But if it is so interpreted, it sounds as if God
is reluctant to answer prayers, which ends up as a distortion of
the passage's meaning. Actually, the context of the verses is
eschatological, offering the assurance of God's vindication of his
faithful.

Beyond the immediate context, however, every passage in the
scriptures is set in the context of the canon as a whole, and again,
it can be enormously helpful in forming the sermon to investigate how the scripture itself interprets some text. For example,
in Jeremiah 2:4–13, the Lord names himself "the fountain of liv-

ing waters" (v. 13, RSV). If we look at the center column references in a cross-referenced Bible, we find the same thought in Psalm 36:9 (RSV), which speaks of "the fountain of life." If we turn to a concordance, we then are directed to the New Testament. In John 4:14, Jesus tells the Samaritan woman that whoever drinks of the water that he gives will find it to be a spring of water welling up to eternal life. In John 7:38–39, our Lord teaches us, "He who believes in me, as the scripture has said, "Out of his heart shall flow rivers of living water.' Now he said this about the Spirit." In short, the living water of Jeremiah 2, which the Israelites have abandoned, is interpreted by the scripture finally to be the Spirit given us by Jesus Christ. Each passage involved may then form a portion of the resulting sermon.

Indeed, the cross-references to itself that the Bible furnishes us reveal a world of riches from God almost beyond imagining. Very often these are presented to the preacher in the form of motifs that continue to be used throughout both testaments.

To give only two examples, the figure of God's ordering and defeating of the chaotic waters in Genesis 1 crops up repeatedly in the Psalms (e.g., Ps. 46:3) and prophetic writings (Isa. 51:9; Jer. 4:23–26; et al.) and in the New Testament (Mark 4:35–41; Rev. 21:1; et al.). Or again, the "yoke" of God is prominent in Jer. 2:20 and Matt. 11:29–30 and other passages.

Sometimes the cross-references in the Bible furnish us with jarring but assuring contrasts. In Gen. 4:10 (RSV), the Lord tells Cain, "The voice of your brother's blood is crying to me from the ground." But Hebrews 12:24 takes up that story to tell us that the sprinkled blood of Jesus in the new covenant "speaks more graciously than the blood of Abel." In a multitude of such motifs, figures of speech, and continuing interpretation and reinterpretation of itself, the Bible conveys the speaking and acting of our Lord. Preachers are called to listen to the whole witness to that revelation as it continues through some twelve hundred years in our canon.

"Faith comes from what is heard, and what is heard comes by the preaching of Christ," writes Paul (Rom. 10:17). In his overflowing love and mercy toward all humankind, our triune God reveals himself and speaks to us and acts toward us through the testimonies of Israel and of the early church that are now preserved for us in the Old and New Testaments. Only through that medium of the Bible can we know Jesus Christ, who works in us by his Holy Spirit to give us wisdom, redemption, righteousness, and sanctification. Only in him, by the action of his Spirit, do we find the way and the truth and life abundant and eternal. We preachers have been called to the enormous and humbling task of preaching in such a manner that the God and Father of our Lord Jesus Christ speaks to our people through our words and leads them into a living relationship with his Son. The one thing asked of us is that we be faithful stewards of such mysteries entrusted to us (1 Cor. 4:1–2).

The Mission of the Church through the Celebration of the Sacraments

Andrew Purves

There are two sacraments, baptism and the Lord's Supper. Some churches include five other ordinances of the church in the list of sacraments, but the Presbyterian Church (U.S.A.) does not recognize these as such. The sacraments of baptism and the Lord's Supper, we believe, were instituted and appointed by Jesus, as this is given to us in the New Testament. Baptism is the sign of our being engrafted into Christ, thus to receive his righteousness, and is the ground of our coming to faithful obedience. The Lord's Supper is the means of our feeding upon him to our spiritual nourishment and growth in faith. Along with the preaching of the Word, it is the primary mission of the church to celebrate the sacraments. Everything else, including all faithfulness in life and ministry, flows from this.

This said, the sacraments are difficult to understand and complex in their practice. Even the apparently simple definitions given above are fraught with questions and subtle nuances, some of which we will have to discuss in due course. Nevertheless, as much as they are intended to secure and nurture us in our union with Christ, they are the source still of damaging confusion and one basis for continuing conflict within the universal church. Certainly the sacraments are a mystery and should be seen as such, rather than as intellectual puzzles. They are modes of God's presence—the tradition speaks of a Real Presence— whereby God through the Holy Spirit joins us to the things of Jesus Christ. We cannot adequately explain them. They are primarily the gifts of God, to be participated in and received by faith with thanksgiving.

But problems arise when mystery unfolds into incoherence. An elder, a grandmother, approached a minister quietly after Sunday service and asked him to baptize her grandson before he and his parents made a cross-country trip by airplane. Unless the child was baptized, she felt, he would be in danger. This is a case of sacrament as talisman. A retired sea captain, living quietly in the highlands of Scotland, never missed church on Sunday morning, but also never received Holy Communion at the quarterly celebration. One communion Sunday the minister was astonished to see him take and consume the elements. A pastoral visit later in the week led to the discovery that the old man felt he was now worthy of the holy meal. Both cases illustrate muddled views of the sacraments. They also suggest a God who invokes fear rather than trust.

Official sacramental theologies and practices also are a source of confusion, often deeply dividing the great Christian communions. One adult, baptized as an infant, at the instruction of his pastor, insists now on a believer's baptism through immersion; another person, baptized and believing, is denied Holy Communion because she is outside the communion of that denomination. When is a baptism valid or invalid? What is the correct way to be baptized? What is required for one to be accepted at the Lord's Table? Who is authorized to celebrate these sacraments, and what happens when this is done? These are not peripheral matters, and any kind of serious stab at ecumenical relations between the churches, let alone unity, will have to deal with longstanding divisions in sacramental theology and practice, and the understandings of church and ordination that arise out of them.

Because this book is written to present the faith of the "confessing" church, representing an evangelical or classical position within the Presbyterian Church (U.S.A.), it is appropriate to say an introductory word also about the fact that contemporary Presbyterian renewal movements seem largely to have become sacramentally "low church." Our denomination has been through a huge liturgical renewal, culminating in the publication of the *Book of Common Worship* in 1993. At the center of this renewal was the recovery of sacramental worship, evident in a significant rewriting of the baptismal service and a reaffirmation of the central role that Holy Communion should play in all Christian worship. Regarding the latter, many congregations are turning to a frequent celebration. Yet the Presbyterian renewal movement appears to be more attracted to contemporary expressivist modes of worship that rarely accord to eucharistic celebration the place that both ecumenical Christian tradition and contemporary liturgical renewal would insist is appropriate.

The grave dangers in the failure to accord a central place for the celebration of Holy Communion include an overemphasis on private experience in worship and a consequent limiting of that which Jesus by command has explicitly given to the church as a primary, regular means of grace. To avoid frequent eucharistic celebration on the grounds of seeker sensitivity, or the like, is to truncate worship for the faithful by denying the people the bread of life. In most cases it also places too much burden on the sermon to carry the full weight of the gospel.

In sum, then, the sacraments are sources of both controversy and confusion. As central as they are to Christian worship, and as vital as they are for Christian growth, it is appropriate again to consider their meaning and role in the mission of the church.

Word and Sacraments

Word and sacraments—these are the constitutive ministries of the church that bind us to Jesus Christ, bring us to faith and obedience, and nurture us in our life of union with Christ. Whatever else the church is, and whatever else it is called to do and say, without the teaching and preaching of the Word of God (and its hearing!) and the faithful celebration of the Word of God in the sacraments of baptism and the Lord's Supper, the church is in fact no church at all. Everything else follows from Word and sacraments.

We signal this "strong" understanding of the sacraments in a number of ways. For example, only baptized persons may partake of Holy Communion. Baptism itself is undertaken only on confession of faith by the adult to be baptized or by those who are parents or guardians in Christ of the child brought for baptism. Ministers are ordained to the ministry of Word and sacraments, meaning that the preaching and teaching of the Word of God and the celebration of the sacraments should order everything else that a minister does. The point is, the church is the church because the Word is preached and the sacraments are celebrated.

Note too that Word and sacraments are to be held together—not Word *or* sacraments, but Word *and* sacraments. Sometimes a tradition will emphasize one at the expense of the other. The Latin tradition of Roman Catholicism, for example, has tended to emphasize the Holy Communion at the expense of preaching the Word of God, forgetting that the Word of God orders and governs the sacraments. The Presbyterian tradition, on the other hand, has emphasized a preaching church, with only infrequent eucharistic celebration—against the wishes of both John Calvin and John Knox. Knox, in 1560, took the communion table from the top end of the High Kirk of St. Giles in Edinburgh, and placed it below the pulpit—Word and sacrament in the closest possible conjunction. The sacraments enact the sermon, as it were, for they are the Word of God given for the people under the elements of water, bread, and wine. The Word of God is not mere ideas, but the living word in both aural and corporeal form. The sermon expounds the meaning of the sacraments, so that they are not seen as magic.

Word and sacraments are central to the life and mission of the church. As such, they are called "the ordinary means of grace" in Christian tradition. This does not mean that they are not extraordinary, or something other than miracles of God's astonishing condescension to come to our level and deal with us here. It means rather that Word and sacraments are the regular God-given means whereby we come to know of God's saving love in Jesus Christ, become united with Christ in his Body, and receive the spiritual nourishment that leads to Christian maturity and faithfulness. Of course God may use anything at all to bring people to faith—in Karl Barth's amusing observation, "God may speak to us through Russian Communism, a flute concerto, a blossoming shrub, or a dead dog"—but ordinarily and trustworthily God uses the preaching of the sermon and the celebration of the sacraments to bring us to and nurture us in faith.[1]

This Word of God in sermon and sacrament is not something alongside God, as it were, something added to God, or something other than God. Because the Word of God is God's living presence in speech and act through sermon and sacrament, this Word of God is none other than Jesus Christ, from whom alone sermon and sacrament have their purpose and content. To speak God's Word is to say Jesus Christ, God's Word incarnate, crucified, risen, and ascended. To celebrate the sacraments is to enact God's saving relationship with us in and through Jesus Christ, whereby we are established in communion with God and grow more fully into that communion. God's Word is Jesus Christ, who is the subject of sermon and sacrament. Sermon and sacrament, we might say, are the form of Jesus Christ for us in this time of the dispensation of God's grace.

Turning now specifically to the sacraments, this is what was intended in the older language of the church when the sacraments were spoken of as signs and seals of our union with Christ. As a sign, the sacraments are not empty markers that point to something else, but they really make present what they signify. With the *Scots Confession*, the church condemns the view that the sacraments are only "naked and bare signs" (*Book of Confessions*, 3.21), mere memorials, occasional reminders, if you will. As a seal, like the President's signature on a piece of legislation, the sacraments confer the reality they designate. They are the "signature" of God conferring surety to what God has promised in and through the sacraments, that we really do have union with Christ in baptism and feed upon him in the Holy Communion.[2]

The sacraments, then, are the God-given outward public enactments of the church (sometimes called "ordinances") that bear witness to the spiritual reality of our union with Christ— both our being joined to him and our growing up in him. Baptism is the basis for Holy Communion, and Holy Communion is the fulfillment of the promise of baptism. They are that important! Note how they are related. But note also that the sacraments are ordinances of the church. They are, as it were, lodged in the church as the body of Christ. A private baptism or a private Holy Communion—sacramental celebrations that are not open worship services for the whole church—are theologically in error in that they turn a communal or corporate event of and for the Body into a private affair. Neither is it appropriate for authority to celebrate the sacraments to be located in an individual "with magic hands." Again, the authority is corporate rather than private or individual.

In sum, in baptism the Holy Spirit engrafts us into Christ, in whom we are born again, becoming new persons. This outward or public act bears witness to the spiritual reality of our lives: we belong to Jesus Christ. In Holy Communion, we are nurtured in that belonging, feeding on the living Lord, completing and ful-filling the promises contained in our baptism. In this way, the sacraments are constitutive of Christian faith and life, being God's way of securing us in his grace. Because of this, they are central to the mission of the church. As such, a nonsacramental faith is not truly Christian faith, but a faith bereft of the bond by which Christ effectually unites us to himself. The sacraments are that important!

The Sacrament of Holy Baptism

A Person Is Baptized Once

A person is baptized once because baptism is an event bearing witness to a reality once and for all established by God, grounded in God's promises and God's faithfulness. God, through the Holy Spirit, binds the person in baptism to Jesus Christ. As the *Scots Confession* states, "we assuredly believe that by Baptism we are engrafted into Christ Jesus, to be made partakers of his righteousness, by which our sins are covered and remitted" (*Book of Confessions*, 3.21). Another way of putting this is to say that baptism is rooted in the act and promises of God rather than in the subjectivity of the believer. That is not to say that the person baptized has no responsibility, for indeed one must come to make confession of faith—although even that is God's work. It is to say that the efficacy and truth of baptism belong to God and do not lie in our affective states or personal feelings about it. It is also to say that baptism is given for faith, not faith for baptism. The classical teaching of the church concerning baptism places the emphasis upon God rather than upon us. This is one significant reason for baptizing infants.

Infant baptism is controversial among some people in the church today, who insist on believer's baptism, citing New Testament grounds. This view is not entirely wrong, but neither is it entirely correct. It is correct insofar as there is a proper place for believer's baptism if a person is not already baptized. In a missionary environment, such as North America is fast becoming, when fewer children are baptized as babies, believer's baptism will become more and more common. Further, as theologians such as Karl Barth and Jürgen Moltmann have insisted, the baptism of children is now so largely an expression of cultural Protestantism, a routinized "rite of passage," that it is often an offense to the true sacrament. The argument is made rightly that the church must exercise appropriate discipline over baptism, ensuring that infants baptized into Christ indeed are brought up within the body of Christ. Baptism calls for the church to be held accountable for the faithful keeping of the promises made at baptism.

But the argument for believer's baptism is incorrect when it means *re*baptism. In fact, the notion makes little theological sense, as if one could die to sin and be reborn into Christ again and again. Our incorporation into Christ needs to happen, indeed, can happen, only once. It is by the secret work of the

Holy Spirit that a person baptized as an infant comes to confessing faith. By a mystery of God's providence not readily explainable, not all who are baptized become believers. For whatever reason, they willfully and stubbornly reject the internal grace of the Holy Spirit. Yet those who do come to faith—and our personal stories indicate a multitude of routes, each one a story of God's grace—are entering into the promises already contained in their baptism. Because one lays active claim later in life to one's baptism is not a ground for rebaptism, but the ground for celebration and thanksgiving that God has brought the promises of baptism to pass.

We are Baptized into the Name of God

Baptism, once and for all time, is administered in the name of the Father, the Son, and the Holy Spirit. We are baptized, that is, into the life of the Holy Trinity, into the communion of the Godhead. Baptism, then, takes us right into the heart of the Christian doctrine of God as one God, three Persons. A non-Trinitarian view of God, and a so-called baptism other than in the name of God (e.g., in the "name" (?) of the Creator, the Redeemer, and the Sustainer) will always lead to an aberrant theology of baptism.

God is self-given for us as Father, Son, and Holy Spirit. Revelation is from the Father, through the Son, in the Holy Spirit, and our response is to the Father, through the Son, and in the Holy Spirit. In this way, who God reveals himself to be, and how we relate to him, is through and through Trinitarian. The Father is the source and the goal, the Son is the mediator, and the Spirit is the bond who brings Christ to us and us to Christ that we might share in his life with and mission from the Father. Further, the God whose saving self-disclosure we encounter in Jesus Christ by the illumination of the Holy Spirit is not some arbitrary mask or projection, but God as he actually is through all eternity. God is not other in himself than the loving communion of Father, Son, and Holy Spirit that he is in his revelation; and who God is in his Trinitarian revelation is who God is in himself.

Baptism is a work of the Trinity through the ordinance of the church: the Holy Spirit engrafts us into Jesus Christ to have communion with the Father through him. By baptism, we are enfolded into the life of God, to share through our union with Christ in the communion of love that is the nature of God. As the New Testament makes clear again and again, it is only through our incorporation into Christ by the Holy Spirit that we come to the Father. Baptism is not just an outward symbol that God loves us or that we are members now of the church. More important, it is the enactment of a reality that we have been named and claimed by God in and through our union with Christ to be God's covenant partners by sharing in Christ's own life with the Father.

Baptized in the name of the Father, the Son, and the Holy Spirit, we are henceforth people constituted by being in relationship with God through Jesus Christ. It is this that makes us persons rather than things. Baptism in this case is the ground of true identity and personhood. To be a person is to relate, and be related to, in love. This is not something just given willy-nilly as a fact of our biological existence. In the love of parents and children, spouse and friends we discover what it is to love and be loved day by day. In this we grow into a deeper discovery of ourselves as persons. But human loves fail, and all around us we experience the wreckage of a world run amok with depersonalization, in which people treat one another as commodities and objects. Baptism is the reality that grounds us in relationship with the personal and personalizing God, to receive our personhood in being unconditionally loved and accepted into communion with God. This is the ultimate ground of personhood, a ground that does not shift with the vagaries of emotion or disposition. By baptism we are engrafted into the personal ground of love as we share in the equal love of the Father, the Son, and the Holy Spirit.

Baptism Is for the Forgiveness of Sins

Here we can be brief and to the point. To be engrafted into Jesus Christ through baptism is, as Paul says, to become a sharer in his death (Gal. 3:3). Another way of saying this is that by baptism we become sharers in the power of his atonement, which means the covering and remission of our sins. To be baptized means that by faith through grace we trust in the forgiveness of our sins. The waters of baptism signify the washing away of our sins.

There is a twofold mystery here that we must hold in tension and that cannot be readily resolved. First, baptism means we are forgiven before we have sinned, but still we are called to repent and make amendment of life. Repentance and amendment of life, which are the gift of the Holy Spirit, are the consequence of forgiveness, not its condition. We often get that the other way around, forgetting that it is the grace of forgiveness that creates the possibility of repentance as the Spirit leads us to see ourselves as we really are in the light of God's mercy. We must take our stuck-ness in sin that seriously! But, secondly, many baptized persons who sin do not repent. Clearly the grace and mercy contained in baptism can be rejected. Baptism, in Calvin's arresting image, can lie neglected.[3] There is nothing automatic about salvation for those who are baptized. The new life given to us in baptism is a life that finds expression precisely in obedience to the imperatives of faith and faithfulness, and failure on that account is dire indeed. The source of tension, of course, is that while everything here is the work of God, still there is a human responsibility. Sometimes tensions like this just have to remain what they are, mysteries that we cannot get our minds around.

Union with Christ Means Union in Christ

The basis for unity within the Body of Christ is not commonality of opinion or shared experience. The basis for unity is that we are "one body in Christ" because we are all united with Christ. United with him, we have union in him. He—and not we—is the source of unity. It is for this reason surely that a priori philosophical axioms like pluralism and inclusivity must not be allowed to usurp Jesus Christ and our union with him as the ground for the church's unity. They are not wrong in themselves, of course. In fact, as moral virtues these abstract nouns have much to commend them. But they are not marks of the church. To insist that they should be allowed to function as marks of the church is blasphemously to undercut the meaning and consequence of holy baptism. Baptism is the ground of a proper inclusivity; inclusivity is not the basis for baptism.

The Sacrament of Holy Communion

Nowhere else in Christian faith perhaps is there as such potential for misunderstanding as there is with regard to the Lord's Supper. What is going on with the bread and the wine, and what happens when we partake of them? These questions refer us to a great mystery that is so much more than an intellectual puzzle. It is with the various answers to these questions that the debates among Orthodox, Roman, and Protestant communions, and even between Protestant churches, get down to very serious issues indeed. It is at this specific point also that the conflict over ministerial orders arises.

The Lord's Supper Is a Real Communion

In the Lord's Supper we participate in a very real communion with the Father, through the Son, in the power of the Holy Spirit. Calvin puts it characteristically clearly: "Our souls are fed by the flesh and blood of Christ in the same way that bread and wine keep and sustain physical life. . . . Christ pours his life into us, as if it penetrated into our bones and marrow."[4] That is to say, in the bread and wine of the sacrament we really do feed upon the living Jesus Christ. In physical feeding, of course, the food we consume is absorbed into our systems. In this spiritual feeding, however, we are absorbed into the food, into the body of Christ that is given us in the sacrament! The elements are not just bare signs, or the Communion a ritual that reminds us of spiritual truths, but they are the means of grace by and through which Christ is really spiritually present for us in a physical medium. Calvin calls Holy Communion "a true participation" in

Christ that leads to our growing into one Body with him, that we may know his power directly and thereby enjoy his benefits.[5]

Now nothing odd happens to the bread and the wine. They do not outwardly appear to be one thing while actually becoming something else. The bread and the wine are and remain bread and wine, the physical symbols by which Christ offers us his body. The mystery of grace in the sacrament takes place spiritually only in the power of the Holy Spirit, not by some metaphysical change in the elements. With this understanding, Protestants reject both the metaphysics of the Mass, with its claim that the elements become actually and physically the body and blood of Christ while appearing to be just bread and wine, and the concomitant theology of the priesthood. The miracle of Holy Communion is spiritual.

For Protestants, then, the singular point of importance is the actual spiritual communion that we receive with Jesus Christ when we eat the bread and drink the wine of the Holy Communion. This is through and through a spiritual joining of Christ and us by an act of the Holy Spirit. By the Spirit, and through the elements, we share in the life of the living Lord Jesus, to receive him into ourselves. Now there is a point to this. The emphasis is properly to be placed on the transformation of the believer through this sacrament, the outworking of the union with Christ to which baptism bears witness. In and through its sharing in the Lord's Supper the church is maintained in her union with Christ. Calvin notes that almost the entire force of the sacrament lies in these words: "which is given for you . . . which is shed for you."[6] The consequence is a confirming of the promise of life in, with, and through Jesus Christ. In this way, through flesh and blood, Christ continues to order the church in its life of deepening faithfulness to the gospel. It is most assuredly on this ground that the case is to be made for the frequent celebration of the sacrament.

The Lord's Supper Grounds the Magnificent Exchange

One of the most glorious paragraphs in the whole of Calvin's *Institutes of the Christian Religion* is the paragraph entitled

"Union with Christ as the special fruit of the Lord's Supper."[7] There Calvin picks up themes found much earlier in Irenaeus (*Against the Heresies*, book 5, preface) and Athanasius (*On the Incarnation of the Word*, par. 54), for example, where these church fathers taught that Christ became what we are that he might bring us to what he is. This is one of the great evangelical, and thereby truly pastoral, insights of the Greek church that became important for both Luther and Calvin. Here we see most clearly what it means that by grace, and in the Holy Communion, we share in our Lord's life before and with the Father as he takes what is ours and gives us what is his.

Calvin insists that we can gain great assurance and delight from the sacrament. The basis for these wonderful consolations arises from the meaning of the sacrament itself exactly at the point where it means that, by sharing in it, whatever is his now becomes ours. What rightly and only belonged to Jesus Christ as the Son of the Father is now ours by grace through our union with him. This leads to the assurance that eternal life, of which he is the heir, is ours; that the kingdom of heaven, into which he has entered, cannot be cut off from us; and that, since we are absolved from our sins because he took them upon himself, we cannot now be condemned. This, says Calvin, "is the wonderful exchange which, out of his measureless benevolence, he has made with us; that, becoming Son of man with us, he has made us sons of God with him." Thus, by his descent to earth, Jesus Christ has prepared our ascent to heaven. By taking on our death, he has conferred his life upon us. By accepting our weakness, he has strengthened us by his power. By receiving our poverty, he has given us his wealth. By taking the oppressive weight of our sin upon himself, he has clothed us with his own righteousness.

The meaning of this is really quite revolutionary for our lives. By the Holy Spirit, through our union with Christ, given in our baptism and renewed continually through the Lord's Supper, that which is ours—our broken, confused, ambiguous lives—is taken by our Lord and made whole, as he offers it to the Father in his own name and for his own sake. And he takes what is his, his own life of perfect communion with the Father, and he gives it to us, so that in, with, and through him we share in his life with God. What is ours becomes his; what is his becomes ours. This is the wonderful exchange that is at the center of Christian faith and life and is the special fruit of the Lord's Supper.

NOTES

1. Karl Barth, *Church Dogmatics*, I/1: *The Doctrine of the Word of God*, trans. G. W. Bromiley (Edinburgh: T. & T. Clark, 1975), 55.
2. For a fuller discussion see Andrew Purves and Mark Achtemeier, *Union in Christ* (Louisville, Ky.: Witherspoon Press, 1999), 23–24.
3. John Calvin, *Institutes of the Christian Religion*, Library of Christian Classics, trans. Ford Lewis Battles (Philadelphia: Westminster Press, 1960), IV.xv.17.
4. *Institutes*, IV.xvii.10.
5. *Institutes*, IV.xvii.11.
6. *Institutes*, IV.xvii.3.
7. *Institutes*, IV.xvii.2.

Truth as Search and Encounter

Charles Partee

Ye shall know the truth, and the truth shall make you free.
—John 8:32, KJV

F ifty years ago, when I was asked to preach for the first time, I assumed sermons took longer to deliver than to prepare. That is not true, because I have been working on this one ever since. In 1950 I anticipated considerable opportunity to improve my theological understanding. This hope remains undimmed today, but perhaps after a half century of reflection I may be permitted to issue a preliminary report on what I see as the main issue: divine truth. This report addresses the subject from the human perspectives of search and encounter with the assertion that divine truth requires divine encounter. I will be using the Greek word *sophia* to mean human wisdom and not, as some today, to refer to a putative goddess. In more technical terms, I am asserting that Christians must not restrict divine ontology to human epistemological limitations. The same affirmation is expressed in familiar, biblical terms this way: Thus saith the Lord, "I am the way and the truth and the life" (John 14:6, NIV).

The Search for the Truth

Like a thumbtack, people are forced into many things, but none of them can go farther than their head. In my early teens I became convinced that if I could just get my head into the Truth, I would become wise and happy. For that reason, I started on a quest to understand the truth—not the truth about some one thing or another but the Truth itself in all its glory. In the little town where I grew up, my older and wiser friends, recognizing these abstract yearnings among my other peculiarities, suggested I should go to a liberating arts college and study philosophy, which is the love (*philia*) of wisdom (*sophia*). This search for wisdom appeared to be the most worthwhile goal for a human life— at least for mine—and I sincerely hoped I would have the wit to recognize the truth if and when I got near it.

Because of my youthful infatuation with Sophia (human wisdom) I was curious to see what her handsomer and more mature suitors looked like; so I tried to locate a real lover of wisdom to observe. Unfortunately no philosophers were listed on any one of our four local yellow pages (I told you our town was small). Thus, I had no good model to study. I supposed that persons engaged in the various learned professions like doctors, lawyers, and teachers might do a little philosophy on the side, but the ones I knew did not seem to devote much time to so vast an activity as the search for truth. Only two groups appeared to have the proper leisure for genuine contemplation. The town drunks had loads of leisure but nothing to say. The second group, the town's ministers, talked a lot about serious subjects, but I thought they were all wimps. My evidence for that conviction was that they wore neckties in their own homes in the summer.

This view changed dramatically when I attended summer church camp. My purpose for going (in those days not yet politically incorrect and socially dangerous to admit) was to discover if the great wide world contained any really pretty Presbyterian girls. To my inexpressible delight I discovered a marvelous number, and many were wonderfully intelligent. It was a great relief to know that such gorgeous creatures existed, and I figured—

correctly as it turned out—that I must be predestined to catch one of these lovely things for my very own, but that is another story. For me the major event, and biggest surprise, of church camp was the staff-camper softball game. Playing third base, I moved in on the first minister, expecting that if the reverend wimp did not strike out, he would hit a weak ground ball. Instead, a wicked line drive about waist high gave me some serious long-term health concerns, backed me up considerably, and caused me to reconsider the ministry as a possible career.

Several decades later I had recognized that hitting a softball is not really a major qualification for Christian ministry, but at the time it was important to me, because it allowed me to notice what a grand old time Christian ministers had when they were together. This turned out to be the shared joy of believers seeking to understand the truth of God revealed in Jesus Christ and serving the community of his faithful. I had not realized that theologians considered all truth as belonging to God, and that the best ministers were interested in not only divine truth but also human truth and natural truth. I was overjoyed to learn that ministers could study the truth anywhere and everywhere and still be doing their job. Therefore, with the intention of joining this noble profession, I paid court to Sophia for many years, enchanted by her radiant, if elusive, beauty.

The Truth of the Search

The search for truth is always obedient, since all truth belongs to God. But our own conclusions about truth can mislead us badly. For example, I never doubted the truth that Jesus was my Savior, but I spent a lot of time flirting with the beautiful Sophia under false pretenses. Specifically I believed divine wisdom was just a continuation of human wisdom. Thus for many years I trudged to philosophy classes at the University of Texas, passing a building on which these famous words were carved in huge letters: "Ye shall know the truth, and the truth shall make you free." I knew Jesus had claimed to be the truth, but I dismissed his claim as some kind of oriental figure of speech. Truth, I thought, was the result of wide-ranging, rigorous intellectual exercise ("no pain, no gain"). It did not occur to me to consider that the notion of abstract truth might be Occidental fiction.

Obviously the place to start any journey is at the beginning, and the search for wisdom gets serious with the great Greek philosopher Plato. A student once suggested to me that Plato refers to a child's modeling clay. In reality he was the first classical thinker whose work has survived for our reflection. It is claimed, rightly I think, that all philosophy is a footnote to Plato. Obviously we cannot discuss Plato as he deserves, but I suggest that Plato's major contribution to the Christian faith was the articulation of a view of God that still intrigues and misleads us. Simply put, Plato and the philosophers and human wisdom (Sophia) teach that God is the supreme ideal of our human aspirations. Accordingly, since human beings have immortal longings, some of them search all their lives to identify and serve abstract ideas like justice, moderation, courage, wisdom. To these classical virtues Plato, that splendid old pagan, added holiness. His dialogue *Euthyphro*, written four hundred years before the birth of Christ, is still rewarding reading. I was not surprised to discover in seminary that many other Christians admired and honored Plato's search for wisdom, because of his evident piety. Indeed Christian Platonism has a venerable history in offering a way of combining faith and reason to produce truth, and its influence is still felt.

I admit that the concept of wisdom, and thus the object of desire, changes over the centuries. Plato's Sophia may be a bit long in the tooth for some hot young thinkers today, but maturity often brings an appreciation for the kind of classic beauty that age cannot wither and changing customs cannot make stale. In any case, Christians are commanded to love God with the mind (Mark 12:30). Therefore, Christians must defend the aspiration for truth that leads to wisdom against all forms of anti-intellectualism. But there is also a danger to which mainline Christians in general, and especially their leaders, are susceptible. That is, we can become so fascinated with intellectual abstractions that we never encounter the risen Lord. Divine and human wisdom are connected, but they are not identical. The truth of divine revelation found in Jesus Christ is not ultimately separated from the truth revealed to human reason in the world, but they are not the same. The difference is that a person may *search* for Sophia (wisdom in the abstract), but one must *encounter* Jesus (God in the flesh). The search for abstract truth offers many benefits, but it does not change sinful hearts. This is illustrated by the fact that looming over the building that proclaims, "Ye shall know the truth," is a University of Texas landmark designed as a monument to higher learning. It became infamous as a deadly sniper's perch when on August 1, 1966, eagle scout and ex-marine Charles Whitman ascended the 231-foot tower carrying high-powered rifles and proceeded to kill fourteen people and wound thirty-one.

The Encounter with the Truth

I am now only a little bit embarrassed to admit how enthralled I once was by the beautiful Sophia, meaning by *Sophia* the search for human wisdom. The worship of Sophia as a goddess I regard as outright blasphemy. The pursuit of wisdom is both good and necessary, but it will break the Christian heart, making a transplant necessary. David recommends this procedure when he writes, "Create in me a clean heart, O God, and put a new and right spirit within me" (Ps. 51:10, RSV).

I was prepared for this divine operation by the fact that before I joined the Platonic search, I was already found as a Christian. My mother had taught me to pray to God's Jesus long before I was old enough to become infatuated with Plato's Sophia. In those days not so many sophisticated knees were bowing before the throne of abstract nouns like relativism and pluralism and diversity. According to Edward Conze, polytheism is very much alive, but the "multitude of personal beings has given way to a multitude of abstract nouns."[1] This means that the popular imagination "is nowadays inflamed by such words as Democracy, Progress, Civilization, Equality, Liberty, Reason, Science, etc." In contrast we simple Christians found our concrete unity in the faith that Jesus Christ was *the* Way, *the* Life and *the* Truth—not *a* way, *a* life, and *a* truth. Thus it was always possible, and perhaps inevitable, that I would some day recognize the conflict between the philosophical idea of truth as eternal and objective and the Christian confession of truth as incarnate and personal and be forced to choose between the Sophia of human reason and the Christ of divine revelation.

I realize now that what changed my life, and caused me to emerge from Plato's cave, was the weekly task of proclaiming the gospel in the church, which demanded a reexamination of my passions. The people in my congregations loved me well enough, but simple honesty required my recognizing that they came to church seeking a divine word (*logos*) from God, not the best human wisdom (*sophia*) I had to offer them. The question then is whether, and to what extent, wisdom can be regarded as mythically born full-grown from the head of Father Zeus or historically as an infant from the womb of the Virgin Mary. What does Athena have to do with Calvary? Should we follow with our eyes the flight of the owl of Minerva, goddess of wisdom, or must we drop to our knees before the cross of the Son of God?

You will have to judge whether I am describing a personal breakthrough or a personal cop-out. I can only confess that I would take the human search for the human truth about God more seriously today if I had never been a pastor in the community of the faithful, responsible for uttering with integrity those thunderous words, "Thus saith the Lord." I believe I was converted to real Christianity after receiving a seminary degree, becoming a pastor, and listening to my own desperate attempts to preach the real gospel to real people in a real church. The theological issue can be put this way: Do human beings aspire towards the truth in heavenly places, as Plato thought; or does the Truth seek out human beings on earth, as the Bible teaches? Is truth found in the absolute abstraction of divine being, as Socrates, Plato, and Aristotle thought; or is Truth found in a concrete incarnation of divine being, as Matthew, Mark, Luke, and John taught? Human aspiration or divine inspiration? Abstraction or incarnation?

I was attracted to Plato's search for wisdom in the first place because of a great desire to know the truth, but it comes down to this: While Plato yearned for a word of God, he did not believe a revelation from God was forthcoming (*Phaedo* 85d). Obviously if there is no real word from the real God, then human beings are allowed to take their noblest thoughts and call them "theology." They can also take the ethical patterns of their culture and call them "Christian behavior." We live in a carnival culture where everything is now a sideshow, but I am trying to describe the One who is standing in the center ring of the big tent. Authentic Christianity claims that the main event in the greatest show on earth is to encounter the Word from God whose name is Jesus Christ.

The Truth of Encounter

When Christians mistakenly assume that finding the Truth is the result of endless search, then the church offers the world a God constructed of the finest aspirations of human beings. In their own way human aspirations are laudable, but a continuing search for God is counter-Christian because Christians believe the real God is to be encountered in Jesus Christ.

Let me illustrate the point this way. In Western society a humanist turn began about the year 1350. After the Protestant Reformation, humanism got a mighty increase from the father of modern philosophy, René Descartes (1596–1650). I well remember during the years I spent in Iowa that academics often complained animal husbandry was more highly esteemed than philosophy. Professors charged that people in farm states put the horse before Descartes. In any case, where earlier Christians were concerned with assurance of divine pardon, Descartes was concerned with the certainty of human intellect. He found his certainty in being unable to doubt that he, the doubter, existed, which is expressed in the famous formula, "I think, therefore I am." Descartes's "I" problem has infected us all mightily, but notice that for Descartes, the reality of God was a cool rational aspiration.

In contrast, Descartes's contemporary, Blaise Pascal
(1623–62), found his "certitude" in another place. We know this
fact because a few days after Pascal's death, a servant accidentally discovered a one-page note in the lining of Pascal's jacket
that had been written eight years before on November 23, 1654.
For eight years, at every change of coats, Pascal removed this
private and personal note from the lining and sewed it in again
by hand. Those of you who know this story have already anticipated part of my conclusion. Pascal did indeed write, "God of
Abraham, God of Isaac, God of Jacob, not of the philosophers
and scholars." But I want to call your attention to the previous
line, which contains the emphatic and ineffable word, "F I R E."
Pascal explains to himself the meaning of "F I R E" by writing in
the margins: Exodus 3:1–6 and Matthew 22:31–32. That is to say,
Pascal, like Moses, encountered the great "I AM," who is not the
abstract supreme being (τὸ ὄν) of philosophic reflection, but the
God of Israel and Father of Jesus Christ. Because we are human,
it is right and obedient to admire the beauty of Sophia. However,
because we are Christian, it is crucial to recognize that human
wisdom is not the foundation for Christian faith. The cool ratio-
nality of logical search is no substitute for the fiery experience of
personal encounter.

Pascal's encounter with God points to and exactly summarizes
what I am trying to say. First, the God of the philosophers and
human wisdom is not the God of Abraham, Isaac, and Jacob
because God is directly revealed in God's Word. Second,
Christian faith and life is based not on the search for God but on
the encounter with God. Therefore, until the church receives
the divine Word, it can offer only a human word. Descartes
sought to articulate the human truth given to reason; Pascal
sought to articulate the divine truth given in revelation.
Christians live *not* by the aspiration for truth in Plato's heaven,
but by the revelation of Truth on God's earth.

The third and crucial point to draw from Pascal's secret
memorial is the conviction that you and I also carry, if not in our
coats, most certainly in our hearts. Pascal encountered the living
God in Jesus Christ. Thus he wrote in broken phrases, "God of

Jesus Christ. . . . Thy God will be my God. . . . This is the eternal life, that they know thee as the only true God, and the one whom thou has sent, Jesus Christ. Jesus Christ, *Jesus Christ.*"

Like Pascal, each of us shall know the truth when we encounter the One who declared, "I am the truth." And the church needs to remember that he added, "No one comes to the Father except by me."

NOTE

1. Edward Conze, *Buddhism, Its Essence and Development* (New York: Philosophical Library, 1951), 41.

Two-Part Invention

Ephesians 5:25–32

Catherine J. S. Purves

Madeleine L'Engle is best known for her fantasy novels for children. Her book *A Wrinkle in Time* is a classic. She has also written a number of autobiographical works. One of these, *Two-Part Invention*, tells the story of her forty-year marriage. It was written reflectively during her husband's long battle with cancer. The term *two-part invention* referred originally to a musical piece composed of two complementary, intertwining melody lines. The title of this book has always intrigued me, because it conveys so well the inherent dynamism and the surprisingly creative character of a loving, faithful marriage.

As she describes the growth and the struggles, the joy and the shared pain, the discoveries and the disappointments of her long marriage, it is evident that it was shaped and safeguarded by the vows that she and her husband took before God. And the love that powers their "two-part invention" is clearly understood to be God's good gift, given long ago, and replenished through the years, as God brought their marriage to fruition.

I'd like you now to consider another two-part invention. This one is also God-given, and God-powered, and built to last for the long haul. This is a benevolent invention intended to shape and safeguard our lives, providing both nurture and challenge, as needed, and forming the framework for a loving relationship that will last unto eternity. This unique Two-Part Invention is God's good gift for us. We know it as the sacraments: baptism and Holy Communion.

It is important for us to see the sacraments as a Two-Part Invention because *together* they represent the internal dynamic of the Christian church. They are not two important things (among others) that the church does. Together baptism and Holy Communion are definitive of the church. They create the church, because they alone bind believers to Jesus Christ, and in that bond, sealed by the Holy Spirit, the love and forgiveness of God are unleashed in power. This is the invention at work, claiming and transforming people, breathing life into the community of faith, bestowing gifts, and inspiring commitment and service.

The interlocking power of this Two-Part Invention of the sacraments is often overlooked, however. In many smaller churches, like mine, the sacrament of baptism is rarely celebrated, while the sacrament of Holy Communion is frequently at the center of our weekly worship. I have noticed that, as the months go by without a baptism, the font is gradually moved off into a corner of the sanctuary. When it is so seldom celebrated, we tend to forget about the centrality of baptism, and we may even begin to wonder why the baptismal font should be given pride of place up front alongside the communion table.

The reality is that apart from the celebration and the reaffirmation of baptism, the sharing of the Lord's Supper is incomplete. To celebrate Holy Communion repeatedly in the absence of baptism is like reading the second book of a two-volume work over and over again, while paying no attention to book one, because the Lord's Supper is just one part of what is essentially a Two-Part Invention.

Another congregation that I once served was thoroughly committed to the evangelical task of drawing people to Christ. Baptism and the Profession of New Faith in Christ were frequently a highlight of the worship. There was genuine celebration as we added numbers to the rolls. But, strangely, the infrequently celebrated sacrament of Holy Communion was a rather drab expression of shared fellowship, lacking any real sense of awe or mystery. Not surprisingly, many of those newly baptized members, who entered the front door of the church in joy, slipped out the back door because their faith was not nourished through the sharing of Christ in the Lord's Supper. They had encountered the grace of God through only one part of the Two-Part Invention of the sacraments.

In the Presbyterian Church we have always recognized two sacraments as essential to our life together in Christ, because baptism and Holy Communion are the two acts that Jesus ordained. As Jesus sat at table with his disciples on the night he was to be betrayed, he said, *"Do this* in remembrance of me." When Jesus was about to leave his followers for his final ascension to the Father, his parting words were, *"Go therefore* and make disciples of all nations, baptizing them in the name of the Father and of the Son and of the Holy Spirit."

These two acts were thus hallowed and set apart from all other manifestations of the life of the church. The book of Acts shows that the early church fully embraced this Two-Part Invention, calling people to repentance and baptism and "breaking bread together" as an integral part of their worship. These acts formed the church, or, rather, through these acts God formed the church, called it into being, nourished and nurtured it, guided and instructed it, protected and safeguarded it. With gratitude the church received these divine gifts and then proceeded to institutionalize them.

In fact, the inherent mystery and the holiness of the sacraments of Jesus Christ are in danger of being lost altogether through this ongoing process of institutionalization. The divine Two-Part Invention has been taken apart and put back together again and again to try to discern its inner workings. We have adapted and reinterpreted the sacraments so much that we have run the risk of reinventing them, often shifting the center of worship elsewhere and turning the sacraments into routine and empty rituals.

When our son Gordon was baptized, I was deeply disappointed by the brevity and the minimalist approach to the sacrament. There was no sense, in the way the worship was led, that anything sacred had happened. Later, after our denomination had voted to welcome baptized children to the Lord's Table, I was again discouraged by the unwillingness of that church to respond graciously in issuing an invitation to the children of believers. They were so driven to keep things tidy and orderly and solemn that they instituted lightning-quick baptisms so that potentially noisy infants wouldn't be in their midst for long, and they continued to exclude children from the Lord's Table, even after our denomination recognized the importance of this as a sacrament for the whole church, adults and children.

When we misuse the sacraments, nothing less than our salvation is at stake. Not that God is limited to these means alone, but the sacraments (along with the preaching of the Word) are the ordinary means of grace through which we are brought to Christ. In the sacraments we do not just participate in the life of the church, or grow in our understanding of God, or remember Christ's life, death and resurrection. In the sacraments we are encountered by the living Christ, engrafted into Christ, united with Christ. A living relationship is established in baptism and then nurtured in Holy Communion through the *real presence* of Christ. If these mysteries are turned into dull or misunderstood rituals of the church, our essential union with Christ may not be established or nourished.

What can we say about this mysterious sacramental relationship that we have with Christ? The letter to the Ephesians likens the bond between believers and Christ to that between marriage partners. "Husbands, love your wives, just as Christ loved the church and gave himself up for her, in order to make her holy" (5:25–26, NIV). This passage goes on to talk about the fact that in marriage a husband and wife become "one flesh," and it concludes, "This is a great mystery, and I am applying it to Christ and the church" (5:32, NRSV).

Our union with Christ, established and deepened through the sacraments, is far more than figurative, or intellectual, or experiential, or even spiritual. It is salvific. The sacraments truly bond us to Christ so that, in effect, we become "one flesh" with him.

The grace and mercy of God in Christ become ours, and we belong wholly to Christ.

Now you may well want to shy away from such a radical interpretation of the sacraments, just as so many choose to dodge the "holy ground" of marriage, which both offers so much and demands that we risk so much. In marriage, once you have truly become one flesh, you cannot again be separate and independent of that love without tearing the body asunder. Yet without that essential unity, there is no marriage.

Without this foundational understanding of our sacramental union with Christ, baptism and Holy Communion are little more than rites of the church through which we seek to enact a memorial to Christ's life and death. Apart from our participation in these holy mysteries, how can we claim to have a saving relationship with him? We must be united with Christ through the sacraments if we are to share his benefits. Yet to encounter the living Christ in the sacraments, to become "one flesh" with him, is to enter the very heart of the Trinity. It is to dare to stand on that "holy ground" where salvation is realized through our union with Christ.

I have read Madeleine L'Engle's book about her marriage twice, and I still can't quite figure out how that marriage worked. It was a strange alliance between two very different people—one an author, the other an actor. They somehow endured repeated separations, serious illness, interruptions and disappointments in their careers, and yet their marriage, that Two-Part Invention, grew stronger through the years. Their love deepened, and their firm commitment to each other never wavered. It's a mystery of God's grace.

We will never understand completely how the Two-Part Invention of the sacraments works to bind us eternally to Christ, how it draws us ever deeper into the love that is at the heart of the Trinity. This too is a mystery of God's grace. We need only faithfully celebrate these holy mysteries, welcoming that encounter with Christ and daring to risk everything in order to gain life everlasting through our union with him.

PART 3

Our Life
in Christ

Justification, Gratitude, and the Christian Life

Stephen D. Crocco

I

When the Swiss theologian Karl Barth died, he met St. Peter at the pearly gates. Eager to see his Lord and his favorite composer, Mozart, Barth was crushed to discover that hell, not heaven, was to be his eternal home. An angel ushered a stunned and shaken Barth to the gates of hell. There Jonathan Edwards met Barth and escorted him down a dreary tunnel to meet a dejected John Calvin and a despondent Martin Luther. Luther acknowledged him with a sad sigh. When Barth asked, "What? Why?" Luther pointed to a man with his head in his hands and said, "Go ask St. Paul." Barth staggered over to ask him, but before he could formulate a question, Paul said, "I was wrong. It was justification by works after all."

To ruin a perfectly good joke, imagine these theologians in hell having a serious conversation about who, then, belongs in heaven. "If justification is by works," pondered Luther, "then the only human being in heaven is the sinless God-man, Jesus Christ, the second person of the Trinity." Barth jumped in, "Because of our sin against the holy God, all of us deserve a place in hell." The discussion took an interesting turn when Edwards asked, "But are we not 'in Christ,' and does not God regard us as if we were righteous? Is not Christ's righteousness applied to us?" "Yes," agreed Paul, the idea picking up steam in his mind, "and therefore we are justified by works, Christ's works applied to our accounts." Calvin completed the argument: "Because God considers us righteous, we are righteous, and we are justified by works—the works of Christ!" The light bulbs went on, and in unison the theologians yelled, "We're free!" Then they picked up their dusty drinking cups and banged them back and forth across the stalagmites until they got Peter's attention. He was persuaded by their argument, and they were escorted to heaven. To run the joke completely into the ground, eliminating any possibility of humor, remember that the conclusions about justification reached by these theologians in this hypothetical discussion were, in reality, among their most deeply held convictions. They should be ours as well.

God seeks out sinners who are alienated from him and who have no reason to expect anything but wrath. God declares them righteous on the basis of Christ's work on the cross. This is the Christian doctrine of justification. It is an act of staggering generosity on the part of God. The miracle of justification is that it happens at all, not whether it happens to few, many, or all.[1] The greatest adventure available to human beings begins when the slate is wiped clean. A teacher of mine used to say, "When I was justified, it was 'just as if I'd' never sinned." After justification, human beings are united to Christ and become part of his Body. Eugene Peterson's paraphrase of Romans 8:29–30, gives a fresh picture of God's plan for human beings.

> God knew what he was doing from the very beginning. He decided from the outset to shape the lives of those who love him along the same lines as the life of his Son. The Son stands first in the line of humanity he restored. We see the original and intended shape of our lives there in him. After God made that decision of what his children should be like, he followed it up by calling people by name. After he called them by name, he set them on a solid basis with himself [i.e., he justified them]. And then, after getting them established, he stayed with them to the end, gloriously completing what he had begun.[2]

The Father agreed with the Son to provide for the salvation of those whom he has loved from the foundation of the world. The Son secured their salvation by dying on the cross nearly two thousand years ago. For these reasons, it makes sense to say that our justification was guaranteed long before we were born. However, God desired to bless particular human beings with the knowledge and experience that Christ's work on the cross was applied to them. Sinners are justified by Christ's work—his life, death, and resurrection—and not by their own works, not even by the "work" of faith. Similarly, the holiness of Christians— which is the concern of the doctrine of sanctification—is possible only in Christ and by Christ's working in us, and not by our own works. None of our works, not even good works done with the "assistance" of the Holy Spirit, can contribute to that holiness before God which is our sanctification. If the apostle Paul goes to such great lengths to teach that we are justified not by works but by faith that binds us to Christ, why do we think we can achieve sanctification by our own efforts apart from him? What follows is a biblical and historical clarification of the doctrine of justification with reference to that question.

II

Over the centuries, the doctrine of justification has been subject to endless qualifications, definitions, and controversies. Regrettably, some of the bitterest arguments in church history are directed against fellow believers on this topic (though, some would say, unless these "believers" get the doctrine of justification right, they are not fellow believers!). Lately, there has been remarkable progress toward agreement among various Christian bodies on the meaning and significance of the doctrine of justification.[3] Denominations that once cursed each other are now proclaiming substantial agreement on the subject. Even some Roman Catholics and Protestant evangelicals have reached considerable consensus on justification.[4] Perhaps these agreements will unite Christians and motivate them to teach and preach the doctrine of justification. The need is great.

Like every generation before it, ours is awash with people,

inside and outside the church, who are clueless about what the Bible says about justification. They seem quite confident that salvation and the Christian life depend on being good enough and performing works of charity. In this popular spirituality, many think that all one needs to do to be saved is to believe in God and be as good as you can. According to such schemes, we are acceptable in God's eyes because God loved us (that is what Jesus Christ showed us on the cross), and in response we try hard to be good. This amounts to putting God's expectations for us on a par with the demands of Santa Claus or an indulgent parent. Do we really think Santa or our parents will leave us nothing but coal on Christmas morning? Will not a God of love save those who try to be good?

The recent popularity of Pearl Jam's remake of the 1961 hit "Last Kiss" gives a spotlight to this kind of bad theology in popular culture. Following a car crash, a last kiss, and the death of his girlfriend, the singer asks:

> Oh, where oh where can my baby be?
> The Lord took her away from me
> She's gone to heaven so I got to be good
> So I can see my baby when I leave this world.[5]

Most theologians would agree that if the singer wants real comfort, he will not find it by doing good works. To be blunt, to rely on being good enough to get to heaven means he'll never see his baby again. Justification by being good, getting righteous by works, relying on works other than Christ's work, is bad theology!

Paul knew bad theology when he heard it. For years, he tried to please God by obedience to the law, and for all appearances he prospered. The apostle was born into a prestigious family, submitted to the right rituals, devoted himself to God's law, and defended his religion fiercely. He worked hard to obey the law, but eventually the law let him down and let him down hard. What happened? Paul discovered the doctrine of justification, or to put it more accurately, the author of justification found him on the road to Damascus. What did Paul think of his works then?

> Compared to the high privilege of knowing Christ Jesus as
> my Master, firsthand, everything I once thought I had going
> for me is insignificant—dog dung. . . . I don't want some
> petty, inferior brand of righteousness that comes from keep-
> ing a list of rules when I could get the robust kind that comes
> from trusting Christ—*God's* righteousness. (Phil. 3:8–9, PTN)

Paul wrote his harshest words when he found teachers who
obscured the gospel by boasting of credentials or insisting that
Christians could gain favor with God by striving to obey the law.
To those in the church in Galatia who fell into this trap, Paul
wrote, "I can't believe your fickleness—how easily you have
turned traitor to him who called you by the grace of Christ by
embracing a variant message! It is not a minor variation, you
know; it is completely other, an alien message, a no-message, a
lie about God" (Gal. 1:6–7, PTN). Paul pushed his objection to
the breaking point: "If a living relationship with God could come
by rule keeping, then Christ died unnecessarily" (Gal. 2:21, PTN).

To illustrate justification, Paul lifted up Abraham, whom we
know as the earthly father of God's people. Abraham was set
right with God so he could join God's plan for the reconciliation
of the world.

> If Abraham, by what he *did* for God, got God to approve him,
> he [Abraham] could certainly have taken credit for it. But the
> story we're given is a God-story, not an Abraham story. What
> we read in Scripture is 'Abraham entered into what God was
> doing for him, and *that* was the turning point. He trusted
> God to set him right instead of trying to be right on his
> own.' " (Romans 4:2–3, PTN)

Paul argued that God is still dealing with human beings the
way he did with Abraham, and he, Paul, was his favorite example. To spell justification out more fully, Paul needed a way to
say how we appropriate the gift of justification. He settled on an
ordinary word that we translate variously as "faith," "trust," or
"belief." In Paul's hands, the word had no ordinary meaning. For
him, "faith" stood over and against efforts to earn justification by
obedience to the law of Moses or any other law. God's promise

to Abraham "was based on God's decision to put everything together for him, which Abraham then entered when he believed" (Romans 4:13, PTN). Fifteen centuries later, Martin Luther relived Paul's discovery that justification came by trusting God, not by piling up works. As a young monk, Luther seemed determined to rival Paul in being good enough to please God, although Luther did so in a Christian context. The results of his extraordinary efforts were bitterness, frustration, and even anger toward God. Then Luther had his own "Damascus road" experience. He finally learned what was pleasing to God and what was not.

> At last, by the mercy of God, meditating day and night, I gave heed to the context of the words, namely, "In it the right-eousness of God is revealed, as it is written, 'He who through faith is righteous shall live.' " There I began to understand that the righteousness of God is that by which the righteous lives by a gift of God, namely by faith. . . . And I extolled my sweetest word with a love as great as the hatred with which I had before hated the word "righteousness of God."[6]

Once free, Luther looked around him and saw ordinary people crushed by the same kind of burdens. His anger boiled against the religious leaders of the day, who had long since departed from the church's best teaching on justification. That teaching had deteriorated into a way of salvation that required works of confession and making monetary gifts to the church.[7] To rely on human works to get us anywhere with God, Luther argued, is to refuse faith, deny Christian liberty, and insult the author of our salvation. That is why he wrote that "we cannot doubt or yield an inch [on justification], though heaven and earth or all things passing may fall. . . . On this article stands all that we teach and live against . . . the devil and the world. Therefore we must be sure and not doubt. Otherwise all is lost, and . . . the devil and all will prevail against us."[8]

III

The doctrine of justification is concerned with how God presents Christ's work on the cross so it can be appropriated by human beings. Paul used the words *faith* and *justification by faith* to bear the weight of the human appropriation of God's gift. Such lofty realities defy description and can become merely a theological slogan for use in preaching and teaching. But words were all that Paul had at his disposal to convey God's plan for human beings. *Faith* has a number of different meanings today, as it did in Paul's day. In a nutshell, Paul's sense of "justifying faith" is as different from "working faith"[9] as night is from day. Working faith is what both Paul and Luther had before they were justified. They tried to please God by obeying the law, striving to be good, and zealously promoting their efforts. Popular sentiments about being good enough to get to heaven fall into this category.

Working faith can easily resemble justifying faith, because it can reject all good deeds except one. What it holds onto is the deed of faith. Although we are talking about faith, faith here is a good work. "I will be saved only if I believe." Substitute "keep the law" or "be good" for "believe," and the works character of this faith becomes clear. The trouble with working faith, as both Paul and Luther discovered, is that it does not work.

What then is justifying faith? In our time, Karl Barth used the phrase to distinguish it from other kinds of faith in the New Testament. Justifying faith, wrote Barth, "knows and grasps and realizes the justification of man as the decision and act and word of God. . . . Faith comes about where Jesus Christ prevails on man. . . . Faith knows Him and apprehends Him. It lets itself be told and accepts the fact and trusts in it that Jesus Christ is man's justification."[10] Justifying faith is the opposite of working faith. It exposes and renounces all human efforts, however subtle, to gain justification, even the effort of faith. What do human beings contribute to the process if not their faith? Paradoxically, they contribute their nothingness, their contempt of all of their efforts, including their faith. Luther spoke of justified sinners as being "naked from all service, works, and merit." John Calvin pictured justifying faith as an "empty vessel." Barth described justifying faith as a vacuum.[11]

Given the empty character of these images, it is not surprising that for Luther the posture of the sinner before God can be nothing other than petition, seeking and begging, and never possessing or earning.[12] I sinners are justified at all, they are justified by the righteousness of God and that, Luther said, "is brought to us without our merits and our works, while we are doing and looking for many other things. . . . For who has ever sought, or would have sought, the incarnate Word, if He had not revealed Himself?"[13] Justification comes by receiving, not by achieving. Luther repudiated working faith because it does not work when it comes to justification. It has no more saving power than good deeds, for precisely the same reason.

Even though human beings receive divine righteousness as a gift, this does not mean that the doctrine of justification is first and foremost about us. It is about God and his gifts, namely and mainly the gift of Jesus Christ. A mark of justifying faith is that it refuses to claim any credit for what was surely and completely God's gift. Here the contrast between working faith and justifying faith is striking. For the sake of clarity, it may be best to say that we are justified by Christ alone. Faith, then, is given to us as a gift to appropriate Christ and be blessed by him.

IV

Unfortunately, the natural human tendency towards working faith resurfaces in the struggle to live the Christian life. Even when they get the doctrine of justification right, something curious happens to many Christians. Gratitude for God's gifts evaporates. Christians forget the miraculous character of justifying faith and return to working faith in the day-to-day Christian life. Commands to pray, read scripture, perform acts of charity, and bear witness to Christ pile up like a stack of unpaid bills. Privileges become obligations. Eyes that once looked toward heaven get fixed in a downward spiral of obligations and guilt. Christians sing hymns like "Come, Labor On," looking for inspiration, and instead they lament their lack of perspiration. Even contemplating Christ's life and death becomes a burden instead of a blessing. "After all Christ has done for me, why can't I do more for him?" "With the Holy Spirit assisting me, is this the best I can do?" When people do not feel close to God, they think they need to do something to get their Christian life back on track. They may become cynical or weary about the Christian life and eventually abandon it. Or conversely, if things are going well and they are doing something right, they may subtly take credit for living the Christian life.

In doctrinal terms, the problem arises when justification is seen as God's responsibility and sanctification as our responsibility. This is akin to "tag-team" wrestling where Jesus wins our justification. Then he tags us and leaves us in the ring to struggle for our sanctification. Karl Barth characterized this kind of Christianity as "All this I did for thee; what wilt thou do for me?" and said the New Testament knew nothing of it. What the New Testament does know is that "in and with His [Christ's] sanctification ours has been achieved as well."[14] Barth continued, "As we are not asked to justify ourselves, we are not asked to sanctify ourselves. Our sanctification consists in our participation in His sanctification as grounded in the efficacy and revelation of the grace of Jesus Christ."[15] Just as justification is based on what God does in Christ, so is sanctification. Both justification and sanctification are gifts, and both are embraced by faith.

Theologians have used different images to show that sanctification is not achieved by us but given to us in Christ. Sanctification, even though we are the ones who have been made holy, is not primarily about us! Phrases like "participation in Christ," "union with Christ," and "adoption into Christ" all speak of a very different reality than tag-team Christianity. Participation in Christ means that we do not simply live with the "help" of the Christ, as though we were the main actors. Rather, we live in, with, and by Christ, who is our Head. Union with Christ stresses that Christ lives in us and we live in him. Andrew Purves and Mark Achtemeier wrote, "As the Holy Spirit unites us with Jesus Christ, his life begins to show itself in our lives. Our action becomes more Christlike and our hearts more loving."[16] Paul described this transformation when he wrote, "The life you see me living is not 'mine,' but it is lived by faith in the Son of God, who loved me and gave himself for me. I am not going to go back on that" (Gal. 2:20, PTN). Adoption emphasizes the organic character of our new lives. In justification God sees to it that we are no longer enemies and strangers to him. But we are far more than just God's friends. We are God's family! Paul wrote these words to the church in Ephesus:

> Long before he [God] laid down earth's foundations, he had us in mind, had settled on us as the focus of his love, to be made whole and holy by his love. Long, long ago he decided to adopt us into his family through Jesus Christ. (What pleasure he took in planning this!) He wanted us to enter into the celebration of his lavish gift-giving by the hand of his beloved Son. (Eph. 1:4–6, PTN)

God is doing a new thing in Christ, and since we are in Christ, we are part of that new thing. "Going along for the ride" may be a useful image to supplement traditional descriptions of being in Christ. The ride image will fail if we think of summer trips as young children, held captive in the back seat of a stuffy car while our parents blamed each other for being lost. If, however, the vehicle is of one of the new super roller coasters, "going along for the ride" has a very different meaning. Strapped in and secure, unconcerned about steering, we are free in the ride. Unlike a roller coaster with its predictable path, however, those in Christ are going places and experiencing things they never thought possible as God reconciles the world unto himself.

It bears repeating: Human efforts can no more live the Christian life than they can earn salvation. The same failures and problems of working faith occur in sanctification when we try to earn it. Think about it. God did not set up the plan for salvation and lavish the gift of his Son on the church only to become a taskmaster. God wants his people to be grateful, and there is no reason to be grateful for rules, guilt, and doubt. "Sanctification by faith" does not mean that we abandon efforts to be holy. Rather, it means that our efforts are set in the context of Christ's work. Christ has taken on the responsibility for our holiness. Paul had no doubt that "the God who started this great work in you would keep at it and bring it to a flourishing finish on the very day Christ Jesus appears" (Phil. 1:6, PTN). We live out our lives as Christians with our destiny settled. Now we are free to live for Christ. The questions for our lives are not simply, or even mainly, what shall we do? but, what is Christ doing? Not, how shall I live? but, how is Christ living through me? There is much hard work ahead, but Christ is doing that work in and through us. What happens to our freedom? To those who have struggled to be good enough, the answer is that we are now truly free. We are free to work, free to obey, free to give our all, and free to do courageous things, all in the confidence that God wants nothing in return but that we be grateful and enjoy the ride.

NOTES

1. The extent of divine mercy is something left to God's sovereign freedom. See Question 49 of *The Study Catechism*: "Will all human beings be saved? No one will be lost who can be saved. The limits to salvation, whatever they may be, are known only to God. Three truths above all are certain. God is a holy God who is not to be trifled with. No one will be saved except by grace alone. And no judge could possibly be more gracious than our Lord and Savior, Jesus Christ" (Louisville, Ky.: Geneva Press, 1998), 12.

2. Eugene H. Peterson. *The Message: The New Testament in Contemporary English* (Colorado Springs, Colo.: NavPress, 1993), 319–20. All passages from the New Testament quoted in this essay are from *The Message*, indicated by PTN after the chapter and verse reference.

3. See, for example, Keith F. Nickle and Timothy F. Lull, *Common Calling, the Witness of our Reformation Churches in North America Today: The Report of the Lutheran-Reformed Committee for Theological Conversation* (Minneapolis: Augsburg Fortress, 1993); Ephraim Radner and R. R. Reno, eds., *Inhabiting Unity: Theological Perspectives on the Proposed Lutheran-Episcopal Concordat* (Grand Rapids: Wm. B. Eerdmans Publishing Co., 1995); and Gabriel Fackre and Michael Root, *Affirmations and Admonitions: Lutheran Decisions and Dialogue with Reformed, Episcopal, and Roman Catholic Churches* (Grand Rapids: Wm. B. Eerdmans Publishing Co., 1998).

4. Although this agreement is heralded by many, there are a number of dissenters and quite a few questions yet to be answered. See "The Gift of Salvation," *First Things* 79 (January 1998): 20–23.

5. Frank J. Wilson, "Last Kiss," 1961. See: www/cosmic-kitchen/Songs/PearlJam/LastKiss.html.
6. "Preface to the Complete Edition of Luther's Latin Writings," *Luther's Works: Career of the Reformer,* vol. 34 (Philadelphia: Muhlenberg Press, 1960), 337.
7. There was not an official and binding Roman Catholic position on justification until the Council of Trent, which met on and off from 1545 to 1563.
8. Luther, quoted in Karl Barth, *Church Dogmatics,* IV/1 (Edinburgh: T. & T. Clark, 1956), 321.
9. I have avoided the old expression "works righteousness" in favor of "working faith." "Boasting faith" would also convey the meaning.
10. Barth, *Church Dogmatics,* IV/1, 631.
11. Ibid., 628.
12. Martin Luther. *Luther's Works: Lectures on Romans,* vol. 25 (St. Louis: Concordia Publishing House, 1972), 251.
13. Ibid., 253.
14. Karl Barth, *Church Dogmatics,* IV/2 (Edinburgh: T. & T. Clark, 1958), 516.
15. Ibid., 517.
16. Andrew Purves and Mark Achtemeier, *Union in Christ* (Louisville, Ky.: Witherspoon Press, 1999), 47.

Hermeneutics as the Practice
of Knowing God

Jeffrey Francis Bullock

*"So faith comes from what is heard, and what is heard
comes by the preaching of Christ."*
—Romans 10:17, RSV

"So, pastor, how do you really know that these words are the
Word of God? What makes these words different than the
words from some other book or novel? How can you say with
certainty that the words contained in the Bible harbor a peculiar
kind of strength, power, and authority?"

Though these questions were never posed to me directly during the course of my congregational ministry, as a preacher of weekly sermons I knew very well that they were real questions nonetheless. They were questions asked by parents whose child had suddenly died, teenagers who were struggling with issues of authority, couples whose marriage was at a very low point. "How do you really know what the truth is?" That was the question and concern, maybe even the hope. How can we really know?

Of course, we are neither the first nor the last generation to ask such questions. Both the Bible and the history of our faith are full of men and women who have struggled in their knowledge of God, people of faith whose certainty sometimes wavered and wandered but who continued to wrestle, trying to understand the complexity and the simplicity of their faith. Over the years, I have come to wonder if the best posture for the believer to adopt is the psalmist's stance of awe and humility, rather than the confident believer's position of certainty and control. Even in our more humble moments, however, there comes a point when the people of God must profess with conviction that, yes, this is the Word of God in all of its strength and power. Questions must be entertained and answers must be given, even if only to ourselves.

The Search for Meaning

Contemporary Christians stand in the stream of a faith tradition that is longer than our memories and deeper than our understanding. Our wants, needs, and concerns, and our attempts to understand the mind of God, continue the legacy of men and women throughout history who have had similar struggles and concerns.

The first place Christians should look for direction and insight into their challenges is holy scripture. But how is scripture to be interpreted? The discipline of understanding and applying scripture, the work of comprehending phrases, words, grammar, and syntax from another time and culture and interpreting them for our present situation, is called hermeneutics.

In the West, the theoretical underpinnings of this discipline were first provided by Aristotle in *Organon* and *On Interpretation*. Richard Palmer points out that "the roots for the word hermeneutics lie in the Greek verb *hermeneuein*, generally translated 'to interpret,' and the noun *hermeneia*, 'interpretation.' "[1] Palmer maintains that these two words point back to the wing-footed Greek messenger-god Hermes, whose function was to take things that were beyond human understanding and to represent them in a form that human intelligence could grasp and assimilate.[2] The hermeneutical ("Hermes") process is thus one in which "something foreign, strange, separated in time, something requiring representation, explanation, or translation is somehow 'brought to understanding'—is 'interpreted.' "[3]

Within the Christian faith tradition this "Hermes process" has taken several significant forms. In rabbinic Judaism, for instance, an interpretive tradition grew up around the task of applying the principles of Old Testament law to practical life.[4] The rabbis' constant drive to integrate scripture into the day-to-day life of the community gave rise to a dynamic process of ongoing conversation and a body of continually adjusted and readjusted regulations that often took the form of oral *mashal* (parable) and narrative.[5] After the classical and Hebraic era, Augustine, in *De doctrina Christiana* (On Christian doctrine), developed a hermeneutic that was designed to interpret the Bible for preaching. Augustine attempted to demonstrate both how an interpreter could acquire a full understanding of the biblical text and how such understanding could be effectively applied and communicated in preaching.[6] Not surprisingly, Augustine's hermeneutical practice enjoyed a faithful following of one sort or another for over a thousand years. Martin Luther, in the spirit of Augustine, clung to the notion that engagement with the scriptural text was a deeply spiritual enterprise corresponding to the spirit in which the text was written, and therefore the interpreter must be informed, consumed, and even exalted by the text.

A very different hermeneutic came to the fore during the eighteenth-century Enlightenment. Rather than spiritual engagement with the text, Enlightenment interpreters sought to guarantee an "objective" reading that strictly reproduced the meanings in the mind of the original author(s). Whereas from Augustine to Luther scriptural interpretation was essentially a faith-informed process that took place within the believing community, Enlightenment interpreters sought to place interpretation outside the believing community, relying instead on "scientific" methods and procedures that supposedly guaranteed the objectivity of one's results. Descartes's famous "truth"—"I think, therefore I am"—was the result of his "pretend[ing] that everything that had ever entered [his] mind was not more true than the illusions of [his] dreams."[7] This turning away from tradition and community, away from faith-informed interpretations that were considered to be subjective or nothing more than "the illusions of [his] dreams," is the distinctive feature of modern hermeneutics. In its place, modern interpreters turned to methods and forms of interpretation that supposedly guaranteed "objectivity." Enlightenment modernity thus supplanted Augustine's reliance on the believing community as the authoritative arbiter of right interpretation. It did this with an appeal to distanced observation and disciplined, disinterested method.

The father of modern Christian hermeneutics is Friedrich Schleiermacher, the dominant Protestant theologian between John Calvin and Karl Barth.[8] Schleiermacher argued that the problem biblical interpreters of his day had to overcome was that of historical distance. Understanding implied spanning that distance, having some kind of internal connection with what was understood. This "internal connection" means "situating the text in the time and place of its composition, as in the logical reconstruction of meaning based on formal analysis and historical research; but it also means retracing the process of composition so that, as Schleiermacher had once phrased it, 'the interpreter can put himself "inside" the author.' "[9]

Both Descartes and Schleiermacher were driving toward some kind of absolute, foundational certainty in their interpretations, but they had different ways of getting there. In contrast with Descartes, Schleiermacher's hermeneutical method demanded that the interpreter understand the author from the inside out, rather from the outside in; from inside an accurate understanding of the author's community, rather than as a distanced observer from outside that community. For Schleiermacher, a person's religious consciousness emerged from "the community life one shares."[10]

In modern biblical scholarship, the term *exegesis* has supplanted *hermeneutics* as the word to describe the contemporary version of Schleiermacher's interpretive process. Gordon D. Fee states that the term *exegesis*

> refer[s] to the historical investigation into the meaning of the biblical text. Exegesis answers the question, What did the biblical author mean? It has to do both with what he said (the content itself) and why he said it at any given point (the literary context). Furthermore, exegesis is primarily concerned

with intentionality: What did the author intend his original readers to understand?[11]

Not surprisingly, in the modern era numerous exegetical methods have emerged that in various ways attempt to understand the "intent" of the author. Most seminary students today become familiar with the practices of form, redaction, and narrative criticism, and more recently they have begun to be exposed to feminist, postmodern, and poststructural biblical criticism. With the exception of a few techniques of biblical interpretation, practitioners of most critical methods attempt to overcome the challenge of historical distance to ascertain the "original intent" or "original meaning" of the particular text.

The question is whether such methods by themselves are capable of adequately sustaining and informing the life of the Christian community. Like the Jewish rabbis, Augustine, Luther, and Calvin before them, believers in every generation desire to know rightly the meaning of holy text. However, when one pauses to reflect, this whole notion of knowing God, of even attempting to understand God, should really be quite overwhelming. Yet, implausible as it may sometimes seem, Christians believe that, through the gift of the Holy Spirit, human beings can come to have a better understanding of God and God's Son, Jesus Christ, by reading scripture. This gift is truly one of the mysteries of our faith.

A Proposal for the Practice of Understanding

In 1998 my wife and I were gifted with our first child; a boy named Noah Henry Francis. From the time he entered the world, we have tried to read to him almost every day. One of my most remarkable discoveries as a new father has been the extent to which an infant's discretionary powers and preferences are developed! While my wife and I expose our son to a variety of stories, we inevitably end up concluding our story time with his not surprisingly favorite book, a little work titled "Noah's Ark." The fact that our child's favorite story deals with his namesake should not go unnoticed. I am learning that egos develop pretty early on! What is most interesting, however, is the way that our son settles down and becomes quiet when the story is read.

Some of the reasons for this are no doubt the sound of our voices, the cadence of the story, and the familiarity of the tones. But the fact that he calms when this particular story is read may also give us a clue to a universal feature of the hermeneutical experience, maybe even our own experience of interpreting scripture. The German philosopher Hans-Georg Gadamer once noted that "words created worlds."[12] Though the horizon of our son's world is still very narrow, the familiar words of the ark story have a peculiar role in shaping him, in forming his opinions, in helping him begin to make sense, to make meaning, of his developing world.

As I have demonstrated, throughout the life of the church, scholars have been writing about how the people of God should interpret scripture. What may not be surprising is that a focus on hermeneutics, on the right means of interpreting scripture, often follows closely in the wake of ecclesiastical controversy.[13] With the advent in recent years of debates around subjects like human sexuality and sexual orientation, attention is again focused on the topic of scriptural interpretation. What is perhaps surprising is that despite the aspirations of their Enlightenment heritage, modern hermeneutical methods have not succeeded in resolving such controversies by any sort of convincing appeal to the "objective" meaning of the biblical text.

Most recently, Presbyterian scholar Jack Rogers developed an important guide, not only about how Presbyterians may interpret scripture, particularly during times of controversy, but also how members of that denomination may interpret their *Book of Confessions*.[14] The guide is a response to a particular dilemma in the larger church. The Bible is, it seems, an incredibly important resource for the people of God, and for that fact we can all be thankful. The problem is that there is an enormous difference of opinion about what the Bible has to say about the particular controversies of the day. Differences in interpretation naturally lead to different opinions regarding God's will, and before we know it, there are charges and counter-charges, hearings, debates, and, finally, overtures to the General Assembly.

Having said all of this, I face a question that is, no doubt, informed by the many faithful teachers and elders with whom I have been privileged to serve over the years. That question is why. Why is the topic of scriptural interpretation so complicated? Why can't the text of scripture mean what it says? Why the debate?

Like most things, the answers to my questions are much more complex than I would like to admit. Interpretation of any sort is a risky business, particularly when that interpretation involves the Bible. For any individual or group to assume that they have cornered the market on what the Bible has to say about a particular subject is, at best, prideful. However, to treat scripture glibly as our own possession, as if it were not a continuing part of some larger history and tradition, is also an arrogance that I fear is particularly prevalent as we enter this new millennium. At this point in our history, perhaps the best that we can hope for is a kind of return to the basics. That is, rather than arguing for a new and innovative hermeneutical method that will either make or break the particular debate of the day, perhaps the church may be best served by recapturing a practice of interpretation that begins with the practice of reading and listening. As when I read a familiar story to our son, I believe that something happens to us and to our ability to understand the meaning of scripture when we are immersed in the stories and the sounds, the cadences, and the plot of the Story.

Practice One: Read the Bible

One of my most enjoyable memories of theological seminary took place at that point in our education where we, as first-year students, were required to take and eventually pass a standardized Bible content examination. As we prepared for that examination, one of my classmates asked one of our Bible professors if he happened to have any advice on how we could successfully complete the examination. "I surely do have some advice," the professor replied. "I suggest that you begin by reading the Bible."

Though my classmate was a bit taken aback by our professor's response, the advice was really quite solid. In any kind of understanding, there has to be a starting point, a base of knowledge, upon which participants may build. For Christians, the Old and New Testaments compose that source of knowledge known as the Bible. As Christians, we believe that there is something different about that particular book. However, if we are to understand the Bible, we must first get to know it. We must assimilate its stories, be aware of various nuances, and have a grasp of the cast of characters. "Faith comes from hearing," Paul wrote, or, in this case, from reading.

Practice Two: Read the Bible Often

This second practice may seem to be rather silly or obvious but, as a point of fact, many Christians seldom if ever read the Bible. This is a tragedy, because something happens to us when we read the Bible regularly and consistently. I am mindful of an elder in a former church who, for forty years, began his day with at least one-half hour of scripture reading. His reading was not directed toward the preparation of sermons or Bible studies. Over the years, he had learned to be subject to, rather than subject over, the text.

This notion of being "subject to" rather than "subject over" a text is similar to what Gadamer has in mind when he describes the concept of play. Briefly, Gadamer is attempting to describe that phenomenon of losing ourselves, of being taken over, of being overcome, by a particular subject matter.[15] He argues that in the process of our being overcome—in this case by the daily reading of scripture—a kind of deep-seated change takes place in us.[16] In effect, through the practice of reading scripture on a daily basis, over the course of time we are not what we once were. The experiences we have at home or in our professions are somehow seen differently and eventually even experienced differently in the context of the biblical narrative.

Practice Three: Memorize Scripture

A number of years ago, I preached a Sunday morning sermon in which a major move in the reflection hinged on a self-critical autobiographical experience in which "I heard the rooster crow" while I crossed a street in downtown Seattle, Washington. As soon as the words from that scriptural allusion to Matthew 26 were out of my mouth, half of the congregation nodded their heads in quiet affirmation while the other half quietly wondered what roosters were doing in the downtown section of the city. I had experienced the generational line of demarcation that exists between believers who were weaned on memory verses from the King James Version of the Bible and the younger generation who came of age at a time when memorizing Bible verses had fallen out of favor. As John Burgess notes, "We would do well to develop disciplines of memorization. Through memorization, Scripture dwells in our hearts, not just on the pages of a book. It can speak to us anytime, anywhere. As we recall the words of Scripture, Scripture recalls to us the reality of Christ among us."[17] Memorizing scripture can serve as an endless resource of strength and hope in a culture that is full of noise but seemingly void of much meaning. If words truly do create worlds, as Gadamer asserts, then a reservoir of words tried and tested by years of practical use will provide confidence, direction, and meaning in our world of competing words.

Practice Four: Read the Bible with Confidence

Karl Barth had a wonderful bit of advice for preachers in his book *Homiletics*. As part of his approach to preaching, Barth instructed his readers to have "absolute confidence in holy scrip-ture."[18] Barth continued, "If preachers are content to make their sermons expositions of scripture, that is enough. So long as they think that practical life requires more, that the Bible does not suffice to meet what life demands, they do not have this confi-dence, this *pistis* [faith], they do not really live by faith."[19] Barth was reacting to a particular kind of preaching that was becoming popular in his day, a homiletical style that tended to place more emphasis on popular psychology than on the Bible. Barth's emphasis on the primacy of scripture, particularly as it relates to his confidence in the Bible's mysterious ability to "meet what life demands," is particularly noteworthy.

Somewhere along the line, many contemporary Christians became almost apologetic about the Bible. Many of the sermons I have heard over the years seemed to draw more from articles in *Time* than from the particular biblical text. In some churches, sermons have become more commentary on the events of the day, rather than a drawing from the deep well of experience and hope offered by the scriptures. Even more sadly, members of many congregations seem to welcome such homiletical practices. I am not arguing for an illustration-less sermon. I am simply observing that there seems to exist in the church a kind of tacit embarrassment with the Bible or a lack of confidence in its ability to be "contemporary."

I suspect that such a position is the result of contemporary pridefulness and, more importantly, our lack of familiarity with the biblical story. As Elizabeth Achtemeier reminds us, "The Christian church is the community that expects to hear God speaking through its Scriptures. It is that community which has been formed and sustained by the God who addresses it through those events and words that are preserved in the Bible. And it is still the community that hears the divine voice uttered through the canon."[20] In other words, the Bible is God's gift to us, and the Christian community can be sustained only by those "events and words" that come from the God who addresses us. Our world is formed by the holy Word.

Practice Five: Share Your Understanding with Humility

If there is one characteristic of Christian piety gone astray, it must be the kind of biblical arrogance exemplified by the misguided believer who knows the words but has failed to absorb the essence of the message. We all have them in our churches, and I suspect that each one of us at times has been guilty. Our certainty of the Bible's witness with regard to a particular situation becomes more confident than it probably should be. The very vehemence and arrogance with which we defend our perceptions of biblical truth sometimes serve to undermine our own claims to be acting as disciples of Jesus. Barth again notes, "Preaching [or sharing] that is in conformity with scripture will be modest. . . . [The] preacher will be under the continuous instruction of scripture, will be contradicted by it, will be kept within bounds. . . . Even after the most arduous study, we still do not really know what to say. It can only prepare us for the situation in which God's Word should be spoken."[21]

The most interesting aspect about this quotation from Barth is that it comes from Barth himself. There is little debate among either his critics or supporters that Karl Barth is one of the pre-eminent theologians since the time of Augustine. For such a theologian to confess that "even after the most arduous of study, we still do not really know what to say" is really quite remarkable.

A confident position shared with the qualification that "now we see in a mirror dimly" tends to leave room for good Christian people to disagree. There is always room to grow in our knowledge of God, and in our attempt to understand God's will for us and for our church.

The Practice of Knowing and Being

The critical point to be made in this chapter is that the church's life-sustaining engagement with scripture involves both knowing and being. The disciplined practices of regular Bible reading, memorization, and humble sharing certainly aid in our knowledge of the scriptures, but knowledge itself is not enough. When an interpreter applies his or her hermeneutical technique to scripture as a craftsman applies a tool to an object, and the process stops there, something is lost. Understanding and meaning, the practice of knowing God, is more than a subject working on an object. As with the impact of the ark story on our son's expanding world, the practices of living with the language of scripture create a world through the medium of words. When combined with regular worship, prayer, and service in community, these practices help to form us to the purposes of God and fit us for our place within God's larger plan for humanity.

NOTES

1. Richard E. Palmer, *Hermeneutics: Interpretation Theory in Schleiermacher, Dilthey, Heidegger and Gadamer* (Evanston, Ill.: Northwestern University Press, 1969), 12.
2. "The Greek word *hermeios* referred to the priest at the Delphic oracle. This word and the more common verb *hermeneuein* and noun *hermeneia* point back to the wing-footed messenger-god Hermes, from whose name the words are apparently derived (or vice versa?). Significantly, Hermes is associated with the function of transmuting what is beyond human understanding into a form that human intelligence can grasp. The various forms of the word suggest the process of bringing a thing or situation from unintelligibility to understanding. The Greeks credited Hermes with the discovery of language and writing—the tools which human understanding employs to grasp meaning and to convey it to others" (Palmer, *Hermeneutics*, 13).
3. Ibid., 12–13.
4. Jacob Neusner, *Writing with Scripture: The Authority and Uses of the Hebrew Bible in the Torah of Formative Judaism* (Philadelphia: Fortress Press, 1989), 1.
5. Robert Brooks, *The Spirit of the Ten Commandments* (San Francisco: Harper & Row, 1990), 1.
6. George A. Kennedy, *Classical Rhetoric and Its Christian and Secular Tradition from Ancient to Modern Times* (Chapel Hill: University of North Carolina Press, 1980), 153.
7. René Descartes, *Discourse on Method for Rightly Conducting One's Reason and for Seeking Truth in the Sciences*, trans. Donald A. Cress (Indianapolis: Hackett Publishing Co., 1980). 17.
8. James C. Livingston, *Modern Christian Thought: From the Enlightenment to Vatican II* (New York: Macmillan Co., 1971), 96.
9. "*. . . dass man sich dadurch in den Schriftsteller 'hinein' bildet.*" Gerald L. Bruns, *Hermeneutics Ancient and Modern* (New Haven, Conn.: Yale University Press, 1992), 152–53.
10. Livingston, *Modern Christian Thought*, 109.
11. Gordon D. Fee, *New Testament Exegesis: A Handbook for Students and Pastors*, 2d ed. (Louisville, Ky.: Westmister/John Knox Press, 1993), 27.
12. Hans-Georg Gadamer, *Truth and Method*, trans. Joel Weinsheimer and Donald G. Marshall, 2d ed. (New York: Continuum, 1993), 4:17.
13. Robert Jenson provides an approachable review of that history where he traces the history of interpretation from Irenaeus's debates with the Gnostics to the historical-critical method of the

nineteenth and twentieth centuries. See Robert Jenson, "Hermeneutics and the Life of the Church," in *Reclaiming the Bible for the Church* (Grand Rapids: Wm. B. Eerdmans Publishing Co., 1995), 89–105.

14. Jack Rogers, *Reading the Bible and the Confessions: The Presbyterian Way* (Louisville, Ky.: Geneva Press, 1999).

15. Diane P. Michelfelder and Richard E. Palmer, eds, *Dialogue and Deconstruction: The Gadamer-Derrida Encounter* (Albany: State University of New York Press, 1989), 78–80.

16. Joel Weinsheimer writes, "This change results from the fact that since the subject is not allowed to act toward the game as an object in itself, the subject does not remain itself either" (*Gadamer's Hermeneutics: A Reading of Truth and Method* [New Haven, Conn.: Yale University Press, 1985], 102–3).

17. John P. Burgess, *Why Scripture Matters: Reading the Bible in a Time of Church Conflict* (Louisville, Ky.: Westminster John Knox Press, 1998), 68–69.

18. Karl Barth, *Homiletics*, trans. Geoffrey W. Bromiley and Donald E. Daniels (Louisville, Ky.: Westminster/John Knox Press, 1991), 76.

19. Barth, *Homiletics*, 76.

20. Elizabeth Achtemeier, "The Canon as the Voice of the Living God," in *Reclaiming the Bible for the Church* (Grand Rapids: Wm. B. Eerdmans Publishing Co., 1995), 119.

21. Barth, *Homiletics*, 77.

The Humor of Joy

1 Thessalonians 1:2–6

Earl F. Palmer

One question about humor always comes up from serious people: Why do we need humor in the first place? I have heard it put bluntly: "Let's just get on with the job, no need to humor us or tell us jokes." This question needs to be faced if we are to defend the humor of Jesus. Is Jesus "humoring" us needlessly when he tells parables, when he gives his disciples nicknames like "Rocky" for Simon son of John and "Sons of Thunder" for the youngest disciples, James and John, the sons of Zebedee? Someone could argue, "Aren't the simple traditional names good enough?" Also it can be argued, "Doesn't this humorous 'new names' practice of Jesus just call more attention to the disciples than is spiritually healthy for them?" Will it not become a possible cause for the dangerous sin of pride? At an even more theologically important level, we could ask if the true solemnity and costly grace of the sacrificial love of Jesus Christ are not compromised by humor.

Humor by its nature has the appearance of an "add on" that is not as vital as other ingredients in any total context of reality. Why should fighting men and women who are at war be assembled for a USO show with Bob Hope and Jerry Colonna in the first place? Such entertainment is certainly not as essential for them as a long list of other ingredients, such as food, proper equipment, training, the latest and best weapons, and strategic planning. The same questions can be raised concerning such an event as the "water to wine" miracle in John 2. Where is the compassion in that sign, since no one is healed of leprosy or blindness? Some could ask if it is even wise to do a miracle that does not appear to be socially responsible from the perspective of a court counselor who has been required to work with the problems of alcoholism and drunk driving. Why is it necessary for Jesus to walk on water in the middle of the night? Does this event have long-term teaching significance?

The parables of Jesus pose their own special problem. Why a parable about a Samaritan and a wounded man? Why not simple, clear, direct teaching about the will of God concerning justice and public aid issues? The parable by its nature is subject to misunderstanding. Why, therefore, would Jesus take such risks in his teaching ministry?

We could argue that the use of humor has the same potential danger as parables. Both run the serious risk of leading us to misunderstand the seriousness of our discipleship mandate. Humor has a softening effect, after all. Is that softening caused by laughter a wise and logical strategy for disciples on a mission to oppose the works of darkness in this age and every age? How does humor fit with the sobriety and the watchfulness that a disciple needs to exhibit in order to live faithfully the apostolic mandate both in the church and in the world?

These questions go to the core of Jesus' ministry, because humor is an inescapable part of that ministry. The humor of Jesus has its source in the joy of Jesus. Is that joy an add-on, a nonessential ingredient tacked onto the reality core, or is it in some remarkable way an essential part of the reality core itself?

This question about joy can be stated theologically as follows: Does joy, as a great word of biblical discipleship experience, have a ranking that can allow it to stand alongside the great evangelical virtues of faith, hope, and love known to us from 1 Corinthians 13 ("Now abide these three . . .")? The apostle Paul gives counsel concerning this fourth word, joy. He sees joy as the natural result of a faith, hope, and love that is centered on Jesus Christ. Notice how the apostle begins the letter to the Thessalonians:

> We always give thanks to God for all of you and mention you in our prayers, constantly remembering before our God and Father your work of faith and labor of love and steadfastness of hope in our Lord Jesus Christ. For we know, brothers and sisters beloved by God, that he has chosen you, because our message of the gospel came to you not in word only, but also in power and in the Holy Spirit and with full conviction; just as you know what kind of persons we proved to be among you for your sake. And you became imitators of us and of the Lord, for in spite of persecution you received the word with joy inspired by the Holy Spirit. (1 Thess. 1:2–6, NRSV)

I believe that the Old Testament portrayal of *hallel*, praise, in the prophets and Psalms is in full agreement with the New Testament portrayal of the word *chara*, joy. In both instances the joy language is interpreted and portrayed as an essential part of love, because love is costly and joyous at the same time. That celebrative core of love is the direct result of the extravagant nature of God's love in Jesus Christ. So we see Jesus telling a parable about two sons to make that joyous core ingredient unforgettable for us (Luke 15). "It is right that we celebrate and have a party, for this your brother was lost and is found." These are not the words of the frivolous friend of a carefree youth who finally comes home from his wild trip to Europe; they certainly are not the words of the angry older brother who has kept track of his younger brother's immoral life. These are the words of a father, the one who suffered the humiliation, the worry, and grief because of a boy who walked out. It is the father who alone bears the cost of welcoming his son home. It is he who invites his other son to join in with the celebration. And what is vitally important for us to hear is that the father assures this elder son of his own belovedness and safety; the father loves both young men: "Son, all that is mine is yours, but this joy is right . . ." It is clear in this parable that our Lord has united joy with love so that the two cannot be separated from each other.

Faith is the portrayal of our trust in the faithfulness of God, and this understanding of faith stretches through the whole of the Bible. This means that faith is not the skill that certain mystics have mastered; nor is it a seven-step process for religious experts. Faith trusts because faith wagers on the trustworthiness of the character of God. The joy in faith comes at the electric moment when a man or woman dares to trust in God and finds that this trust is validated in spite of the contradictions that were there early on during the time of deciding.

The joy of our discovery of the faithfulness of God must not be eliminated from the core experience that the Bible calls faith in God. It is like the joy that floods two lovers when a young man speaks the promise and commitment of love and then asks the woman he loves how she feels about his proposal. If she hugs him tightly and says, "I love you too; yes, I want to marry you," then they experience together a joy that surpasses even the strong sexual and emotional desire of attraction. Such joy is an essential part of the goodness of faith. Faith in the one who deserves our trust is joyous just because it is so good and right. Jesus put it this way: "Take my yoke upon you. . . . For my yoke is easy, and my burden is light" (Matt. 11:29–30, NRSV).

Hope is the assurance here and now that comes toward believers in the present, but it comes from the future. It is our assurance that the God whom we meet in our present journey of faith is the same one who reigns in the future. This assurance has the identical joy that is a part of love and faith, because of the goodness of the one whom we will meet in that future.

Karl Barth explained the joy of this expectation clearly and simply: "There are no major surprises for a Christian believer when we die. We meet the same Jesus Christ at the end of history as we have come to know at the middle of history."[1] Since it is Jesus Christ whom we meet at the boundary of life and death, we have the best of all reasons to rejoice in our hope. Hope and joy therefore cannot be separated in the life of a Christian.

The humor of Jesus is an ally of joy, and therefore joy is not an extraneous add-on to greater realities. There are no greater realities. We are given permission to enjoy the rich humor of the

Bible, but it is not only the humor that graces the recipient of this good news about joy! We can now understand the energy of the Christian life. If you or I feel that odd fatigue that comes in upon us from fear or boredom or disobedience, or from the disappointments with ourselves or others, we now know where a cure is possible. The cure to fatigue is the joy that naturally follows faithfulness, love, and hope. This is why Jesus could say in truth that his "yoke is easy." This is because our obedience to his will for human life produces not fatigue but energy, even a sense of humor.

Music benefits, too! The celebrative, joyous, and contemplative songs of faith are not luxuries for the rich; they have a secure home in Christian faith, just as humor does. I believe that music and the songs of faith have the same essential source of meaning in the Christian journey as humor. There may be those of a serious frame of mind who do not agree. Some think that pipe organs and guitars, poets, dancers, actors, and singing groups should not take up so much space or time in the church of Jesus Christ. But these worriers and non-singers "will need to take a crash course to really fit in when they get to heaven if we are to believe that Bible's portrayals of heaven" (Walt Hearn, poet and scientist). Hell is the really serious future place to be, because there is absolutely nothing to laugh, dance, or sing about in that lonely place where, as C. S. Lewis described it, "each person is at an infinite distance from every other person." But heaven will be the place of song and holy laughter (Revelation 5, Luke 15).

We owe the next generation not only a legacy of social and human concern for justice, for love, for faithfulness to truth, for hope. We also owe a legacy of joy, and that is where our collection of hymns and folk songs and poems fits in. It is where music of all kinds, drums, dance costumes, theaters and sports, peaceful times of human fellowship, games for fun, and the humorous stories we tell also have their place. It is one strong argument for the joy of beauty, and for the grand cathedrals that lift our eyes when we walk in and surround us with the stained glass of God's faithful story. We humans instinctively begin to speak more softly when we enter a cathedral, and that quiet joy of wonder should be a part of the experience, if possible, of every man and woman, every girl and boy. We owe it to them.

This is also why we owe it to the world and to the people of faith to keep real pipe organs in churches. This marvelous instrument of pipes, reeds, chimes, and wind was born in the church, and it is the grand instrument of joy. It can play more softly than any other musical invention; and when it is loud, it is able to shake a building. We owe this instrument, with its sense of wonder and sense of humor, to the future generation..

I remember attending a concert when I was a university student during which a large university choir and orchestra were presenting "The Battle Hymn of the Republic." During the final stanza I began to feel a profound underpinning, and then gradually more and more I became aware of a power and a depth of bass notes joining in with the chorus and orchestra. Then I saw it. In that concert hall the great pipe organ had entered the song; at first with such subtlety that it seemed as if flute and horn players far away were gradually coming near. By the time the final notes of that hymn were sung with full choir and orchestra and full, mighty pipe organ, my heart had melted, and tears were streaming down my face. It was the sheer joy of the good song of music to the glory of God. I want that joy for every girl and boy, young woman and young man, grandmother and grandfather. I want it to take them by surprise as it did me; I want them to be able to cry because it is so beautiful and well-pleasing, too.

We are told that there will be such a day, when the greatest chorale of all time will be sung with a vast choir, and you can be sure the organists and the drummers and the guitarists and the dancers and the poets and the ice skaters and the farmers and the scholars and the workers in the factories and their children will be there, doing what they do best to the glory of God. The song will be "Worthy is the Lamb" (Rev. 5:12).

We also owe future generations humor. Humor is the story that joy tells. G. K. Chesterton put it best of all: "I have often thought that the gigantic secret of God is his mirth." We humans need the mirth of Jesus, not to be humored, but to become more human—which is one thing that humor does to us and for us and in us. The humor of joy draws us near to Jesus so that we want to trust him more. We owe this humor to our children because, however serious and heavy life is and can become, the greatest truth of all still is this, that Jesus Christ who gave his life for our salvation is alive, really alive. The tomb is empty because a real victory has been won over death, over sin, and over evil. Therefore the word that pleases us more than all the other words is joy. Paul said it well in one of his most humorous lines, "Where sin increased, grace increased more" (Rom. 5:20, NIV). How is this possible? It is because of Jesus, who began his ministry at the River Jordan alongside a very serious and earnest man called John the Baptist. But then by total surprise God spoke, "This is my beloved Son, with whom I am well pleased" (Matt. 3:17, RSV).

NOTE

1. Karl Barth, *Dogmatics in Outline*, trans. G. T. Thomson (New York: Philosophical Library, 1945), 131, 133.

The Invincible Word

Isaiah 55:1–13

B. Clayton Bell, Sr.

Indeed, the word of God is living and active, sharper than any two-edged sword, piercing until it divides soul from spirit, joints from marrow; it is able to judge the thoughts and intentions of the heart.
—Hebrews 4:12, NRSV

A teacher took her fifth-grade class to the zoo for a field trip one beautiful spring day. Many of the children had never been to the zoo and were absolutely fascinated by the exotic wild animals that they previously had seen only in pictures but were now seeing live.

However, there was one boy in the class who had been to the zoo before. He acted rather bored by the excursion, and by nature he seemed an obnoxious pest. His main interest was in making others—especially his teacher—miserable. She had put up with his behavior all year and had developed a certain immunity to his obnoxiousness.

When the class got to the lions, all of them were duly awed by the king of beasts. All, that is, except one. Somewhere along his stroll through the zoo, the pest had picked up a long stick, and now proceeded to try to impress his classmates with his attack on the lion through the bars. As if that weren't enough, he picked up a small stone and threw it at the lion.

About that time one of the lion keepers happened by, and seeing the boy provoking the lion, he stepped protectively between the boy and the cage and said, "Stop! Don't pester the lion." With that, a voice, which sounded suspiciously like the teacher's, was heard from the back of the crowd, "Don't defend the lion. Just turn him loose."

Some Christians feel the Bible has to be defended. One such person wrote a book titled *In Defense of the Bible*. While I applaud his intention, I want to suggest to you that the Bible doesn't so much need to be defended, as *it needs to be turned loose*.

Sometime in the late 1920s, Robert S. Burris, a Presbyterian missionary to China, set out on a ninety-five-mile trip to Wang Chow. There he was to set up a new mission station. In addition to his personal items, his luggage contained two thousand copies of the New Testament. On the afternoon of the first day, two men leading a beautiful dapple-gray pony approached him and his Chinese helper. One of the men said, "An esteemed missionary like you should not be walking. You ought to be riding this lovely pony, and we will be glad to sell him to you for only $50."

Mr. Burris thanked them for their generous offer, but said he didn't have $50.

"We'll let your have him for $40," said one of the men.

"Thank you," replied Mr. Burris, "but I don't have $40."

The man with the donkey kept lowering the price until he reached $15. However, Mr. Burris still did not have the necessary funds.

That night, Mr. Burris and his helper stopped at an inn for the night. When morning came, they continued their journey. But they had not gone far when they were stopped by armed robbers. Mr. Burris recognized two of the bandits as the men who had tried to sell him the pony the day before, and then their strategy dawned on him. They were trying to find out how much money he had in his possession, with the intention of robbing him the next day and recovering their pony as well.

When the robbers found only eighty cents in cash, they threatened to behead Mr. Burris on the spot. Mr. Burris explained to them that they could get as much from him with his head attached as with it detached. He only had eighty cents, and it was not necessary to remove his head to get it.

The bandits left, and that night, as Mr. Burris and his helper lay down to sleep, they wondered what would happen to the two thousand copies of the New Testament that had been stolen. They prayed that God would in some way bless those scripture portions, and, as Mr. Burris wrote, "I claimed God's promise in Isaiah 55:11, '*My word . . . will not return to me empty, but will accomplish what I desire and achieve the purpose for which I sent it*' " (NIV).

Time passed, and Mr. Burris forgot about that incident. Twenty-five years later, having been forced to return to the United States because of ill health, he was serving as pastor of a Presbyterian church in Canton, Ohio, living right across the street from the pastor of a church of another denomination. His neighbor came over to him one day with an invitation. "This Sunday evening we are going to have a missionary from China speak, and we would like for you to meet each other. Won't you come hear him?" Mr. Burris accepted.

The missionary had been located about three hundred miles from where Mr. Burris had served. He showed slides of his work, and one picture was of a church 150 miles from where Mr. Burris had served. The church was a crudely built bamboo structure that would seat nearly four hundred people, and the visiting missionary explained that it was called "The Miracle Church." He said, "When the first Christians went into the area to do evangelistic work, they found this church with four hundred members, and no Christian worker had been here before. Furthermore, every church member had a copy of the New Testament, and we have no idea where they came from." But Mr. Burris knew.

This is what happens when the Word of God is turned loose. The writer of Hebrews wrote, "For the word of God is full of living power. It is sharper than the sharpest knife, cutting deep into our innermost thoughts and desires. It exposes us for what we really are" (4:12, NLT). The Bible, because God inspired its writing, is a dynamic book. God stands behind its message, and that message reveals our sinfulness and the remedy for our sin.

Who ought to read the Bible?

Why read the Bible?

Who profits from the Word? After all, not everyone who reads it has a life-changing experience. I have known people who, like the Pharisees in Jesus' day, became experts in the Bible. But their knowledge of biblical content did not change their lives and was not translated into their relationships and responsibilities.

I

Isaiah gives us a clue in certain words he uses to identify the ones to whom God extends this gracious invitation. "Come, all you who are thirsty, come to the waters; and you who have no money, come, buy and eat! Come, buy wine and milk without money and without cost. Why spend money on what is not bread, and your labor on what does not satisfy? Listen, listen to me, and eat what is good, and your soul will delight in the richest of fare" (Isa. 55:1–2, NIV).

Jesus offered us a variation on this theme when he said, "Blessed are those who hunger and thirst for righteousness, for they will be filled" (Matt. 5:6, NIV).

People who hunger and thirst for righteousness will find their cravings satisfied through reading the written Word of God.

II

Many years ago, Augustine of Hippo wrote words that described not only his own hunger and thirst for God, but the homesickness of all persons separated from God. "Thou hast created us for thyself, and our hearts are restless until they find their rest in thee."

In Isaiah's words, "Seek the LORD while he may be found; call on him while he is near" (Isa. 55:6, NIV). To whom are these words directed? They are directed to those who are separated from God.

It is through the message of the Bible that the hunger and thirst of the soul are satisfied as the Bible leads to Jesus Christ. In Jesus' parable about the prodigal son, he tells about a boy who willfully leaves home, squanders his inheritance, ends up feeding pigs, and then decides he would be better off as one of his father's hired hands. His motive may have been selfish, but his hunger for something better led him in the right direction, and he discovered a gracious welcome back into the family where he belonged.

People who are lost and homesick for God ought to read the Bible because it tells them how to find the way home.

III

Isaiah continues: "Let the wicked forsake his way and the evil man his thoughts. Let him turn to the LORD, and he will have mercy on him, and to our God, for he will freely pardon" (Isa. 55:7, NIV).

How do the wicked know the Lord will have mercy? What assurance do sinners have that the Lord will pardon?

The writer of Hebrews said that "in the past God spoke to our forefathers through the prophets at many times and in various ways, but in these last days he has spoken to us by his Son" (Heb. 1:1–2, NIV).

God has spoken. He has revealed himself in nature, in the human conscience, by direct inspiration to prophets, and supremely in the person and work of Jesus Christ. It is his Word spoken to us in Jesus Christ, recorded in the Bible, that gives us the good news of salvation.

People who know they are sinful and guilty and who want to find mercy and forgiveness ought to read the Bible because it tells them about the God who is merciful and forgiving and about Jesus, who died in their place to purchase their forgiveness.

IV

Isaiah continues: " 'For my thoughts are not your thoughts, neither are your ways my ways,' declares the LORD. 'As the heavens are higher than the earth, so are my ways higher than your ways and my thoughts than your thoughts' " (Isa. 55:8–9, NIV).

It is clear from these words that God lives and views our life from a completely different perspective from ours. If we want God's point of view, we need help. Therefore, *people who want to understand life and eternity from God's point of view must read the Bible in order to get his perspective.*

Are you beginning to get the picture? The Bible is not profitable for the idly curious . . . nor for the religious hobbyist . . . nor for the determined skeptic.

The Bible is profitable for the spiritually famished . . . for the spiritually homesick . . . for the guilty sinner . . . for the earthbound believer who longs to see how God sees the world.

The *Westminster Confession of Faith* says in chapter 1: "Although the light of nature, and the works of creation and providence, do so far manifest the goodness, wisdom, and power of God, as to leave men inexcusable; yet are they not sufficient to give that knowledge of God, and of his will, which is necessary unto salvation; therefore it pleased the Lord, at sundry times, and divers manners, to reveal himself, and to declare that his will unto his Church; and afterwards for the better preserving and propagating of the truth, and for the more sure establishment and comfort of the Church against the corruption of the flesh, and the malice of Satan and the world, to commit the same wholly unto writing" (*Book of Confessions*, 6.001).

The purpose of the Bible is to fill in the blanks left by natural revelation and providence. Nature declares God as the almighty Creator. Conscience declares God to be a moral being and the judge. But only the Bible reveals that God is Savior! God has given us a divinely inspired, authoritatively accurate written record of himself, culminating in his incarnation in the person of Jesus Christ, the Living Word. In this record he teaches us what he wants us to believe about himself and what duty he requires of us.

I don't know a better expression of this than that found in the second and third stanzas of William Walsham How's great hymn "O Word of God Incarnate":

> The church from her dear Master received the gift divine,
> And still that light she lifteth, o'er all the earth to shine.
> It is the golden casket, where gems of truth are stored;
> It is the heaven-drawn picture of Christ, the Living Word.

It floateth like a banner before God's host unfurled;
It shineth like a beacon above the darkling world.
It is the chart and compass that o'er life's surging sea,
'Mid mists, and rocks and quicksands, still guides, O Christ,
to thee.

In the mid-1950s, a Dutchman known only as Brother Andrew
started a unique ministry of smuggling Bibles into Communist
countries. His first book, *God's Smuggler*, was written to
describe his ministry. One story in his book stands out in my
memory. In the fall of 1956 hundreds of thousands of terrified
and disillusioned people fled during the Hungarian Revolt. The
refugees were herded into vast camps near the border where
conditions were unthinkable.

Brother Andrew responded to a plea for volunteers to help in
the camps. He discovered that most of the refugees knew literally nothing about the Bible. Persons who had grown up under
the old regimes were largely illiterate. The younger generation
had been raised under communism and was better educated, but
of course not in the Bible. Brother Andrew began working
through an interpreter to hold a few small classes in the most
basic kind of Bible education. Let me quote:

I knew from experience how powerful this knowledge can
be, but I was scarcely prepared for its effect on lives in which
it was totally new. People who had sunk in despair became
pillars of strength for a whole barracks. I saw bitterness
change to hope, shame to pride.

I remember one old couple, escapees from Yugoslavia.
The wife was smelly and fat and had chin hairs an inch long.
She at least tried to keep the area around their beds picked
up and tidy, but her husband, unsettled by the move from his
ancestral farm, just sat on the edge of his cot, rocking endlessly back and forth day after day.

They began attending the Bible class I taught in their barracks. At first they appeared thunderstruck at what they heard.
The old man wept as he listened, letting tears fall unchecked
into his lap. By the fourth class I noticed that the woman's
chin hairs were gone, and the husband had begun to shave.

Tiny details, of course. Except for what they said about two people awakening to a sense of themselves as beloved children of God.[1]

One of the major personality problems of today is the problem of low self-esteem. How do we improve our self-image? How do parents improve the self-image of their children?

The Bible has the answer. The Bible tells us that we are created in the image of God and are important to God. We are on this earth by divine design, not by chance. Although we are so bad that God had to send His Son, Jesus, to die for our sins, we are so valuable to God that God was willing to pay the price of his Son to redeem us.

V

One final thing we learn from this passage in Isaiah is that the Word of God has power: "It shall accomplish that which I purpose and prosper in the thing for which I sent it" (Isa. 55:11, RSV).

Was it a preacher who went into that Chinese community and produced four hundred Christians in a thriving church? No. It was the printed Word of God that had power to convert unbelievers into believers and to build a church.

Don't get bogged down in debates about the nature of the inspiration and authority of the scriptures. Read them! Ask God's Holy Spirit to reveal the truth you are to believe and by which you are to live. Turn it loose in your life! Give it a chance to satisfy your hungry soul . . . to show you the path home . . . to lead you to the mercy and forgiveness of God . . . to give you heaven's perspective on this earthbound pilgrimage on which we all are traveling.

NOTE

1. From *God's Smuggler*, by Brother Andrew, with John and Elizabeth Sherrill (New York: New American Library, 1967).

PART 4

Christ's
Life in Us

The Call to Holiness

Margaret Kim Peterson

I

"You shall know the truth, and the truth shall make you odd"—or so Flannery O'Connor is reputed to have said. In the midst of the sad and broken world we inhabit, holiness can indeed look very strange. Perhaps this is why God's call to holiness so often meets with incomprehension and resistance, even from those whom God has drawn to himself in Christ. We are so used to our sins, and to the sins of others, that we are tempted to think that they are normal. In fact, this is precisely the predicament of sinful human beings: our alienation from God is so fundamental that we cannot even see that there is a problem. We do not just need forgiveness; we need change. We need to be renewed in our minds and hearts and souls and bodies, and made able to love and serve God and to love and serve one another and all creation as God would have us love and serve them.

This is what holiness is. Through the redemption that God has accomplished in Christ, humans are called and enabled to be holy, to be set apart for the purposes of God. According to Christian teaching, the very reason that God became a human being was so that humans might be like God, with characters and relationships that reflect God's character and relationships.

129

Catholic Christians have traditionally understood the justification of the Christian to include both God's forgiveness of the person and the actual holiness that God has brought about in that person's life. Protestant Christians understand justification as the right standing before God that God gives to those who are in Christ, and give a different name, sanctification, to the holiness that God brings about in the life of the Christian.

For Protestant and Catholic alike, holiness is an intrinsic element of the Christian life, as God adds renewal to forgiveness and causes us increasingly to grow into his image and likeness. Holy living is a part of God's redemptive work, in which God invites our active participation. God is sovereign in all of redemption, and there are some elements of salvation that are entirely his doing, for example, the life and death of Jesus on our behalf. Jesus' saving life and death is not something to which we can contribute; it is rather something that God does for us, and that we can only gratefully receive, as God works repentance and faith in us. In the Christian life, however, we are involved not only as recipients but also as participants. "Work out your own salvation with fear and trembling; for God is at work in you, both to will and to work for his good pleasure," says Paul (Phil. 2:12–13, RSV). In sanctification, God continues his work of redemption, as the Holy Spirit renews us from within, forming us into the likeness of Christ by our union with him. This inward renewal enables us to live in ways that reflect our union with God and thus increasingly to cooperate with God in his redemptive work.

The active participation of believers with God in holy living is part of the reason the Christian life is understood as one of freedom. A Christian is no longer a slave to sin; rather, he or she is free to do the will of God in love. Christian freedom is thus not an absence of all constraint. Christian freedom is "slavery to righteousness," that is, to God (Rom. 6:18). This seeming paradox is rooted in the reality that humans are intrinsically worshiping, serving, loving beings. The sad reality of sin is that we have turned from the worship and love of God to the worship and love of that which is not God. In Christ, we are freed from the worship of our false gods for the worship of the true God. The alternatives with which humans are confronted in this world are not slavery to sin on the one hand, and some sort of absolute freedom on the other. Our choice is between two masters, sin on the one hand, and God on the other. In Christ, God frees us from sin and unites us, instead, to himself, "whose service is perfect freedom," as the Anglican *Book of Common Prayer* puts it.

Holiness thus has to do with service, with obedience. Jesus lived a life of perfect obedience to God, and we too are called to lives of obedience to our heavenly Father. We are guided in this obedience by the moral requirements of God. These moral requirements include the specific commandments and prohibitions of scripture, understood within the overarching story of redemption of which they form a part. Holy living is thus more than a matter of doing things the Bible commands, and not doing things the Bible prohibits. Holy living has to do, through our union with Christ, with being like Jesus, with having our selves and our actions reflect the character of God. That goes much further, and much deeper, than any finite number of biblical commands ever could. Jesus teaches us that it is not enough to avoid adultery; we must repent of lust as well (Matt. 5:27–28). Simple adherence to God's commandments is only the beginning of holiness. True Christian righteousness involves the renovation of our whole selves in light of Christ.

On the other hand, adherence to God's commandments *is* the beginning of holiness! The specific commandments of scripture give us a concrete indication of what holy behavior is going to look like. Sometimes it can be tempting to suppose that the love of God and neighbor to which Christians are called is somehow self-evident, that we can figure out for ourselves what constitutes loving action in any given situation. But as long as we are incompletely renewed, which is to say, as long as we are in this life, we need assistance in perceiving and understanding how we are to love God and one another. Our love for God and neighbor is therefore to take the concrete form of obedience to God's commandments, both in their specifics and in their wider implications. Christ's obedience to the Father is our pattern and our goal, and it is through our union with Christ that we are able increasingly to understand and obey the commandments of scripture as the Holy Spirit works in our lives to bring us into closer and closer conformity to that obedience.

Christians grow in holiness both as we repent of and cease from sin and as we embrace and practice obedience to God. Scripture uses the language of life and death to describe these processes. "You also must consider yourselves dead to sin and alive to God in Christ Jesus," says Paul (Rom. 6:11, RSV). We are to put to death our sinful actions and desires and to be renewed and made alive in holiness (Col. 3:5; Eph. 4:23–24). Another set of metaphors employs the language of warfare. Holy living is a battle fought against the powers of spiritual darkness. If Christians are to prevail, they must enter the battle armed with all the weaponry that the gospel has to offer (Eph. 6:11–17). This is vivid and dramatic language, and our experiences of repentance and holy living may sometimes be vivid and dramatic as well. At other times, our experience may be more that of a long, slow slog, fraught with missteps and discouragement. Whatever the character of our experience, however, to cease from sin and embrace holiness is to participate with God in the great drama of redemption.

This drama is one that will be complete only at the last day, when all things find their consummation in Christ. Our participation in that drama will find its fulfillment only then, as well. Holy living is a process that in this life will always be ongoing. Even though Christ has won a decisive victory over sin, we do not yet see the final accomplishment of that redemption. For Christians as individuals, and for the church as a whole, this means that in this life we are always both justified and sinners. We are justified by the blood of Christ; but we are still sinners who need grace, and whose repentance needs to deepen daily, as God works to renew us from within. This transforming activity of the Holy Spirit is a sign that God is indeed at work in us, and a promise that he will finally complete that work in the life to come. This promise helps us to hope for that completion, even when the continuing reality of sin and the continuing need for repentance threaten to dismay us.

We can compare the process of sanctification to the process of cultivating a field in New England. The soil of New England is rocky, and so the first year that a farmer cultivates a field, he or she picks up all the rocks on the surface of the field, makes a fence with them, and plants the field. The next year, there are more rocks in the field. This is not because the farmer intentionally, or even inadvertently, left rocks in the field. It is because the freezing and thawing of the earth has caused to rise to the surface certain rocks that before were hidden. So the farmer adds those rocks to the fence and plants the field again. The next year, there are more rocks again. In fact, there are more rocks every spring. The farmer cannot remove them all at the beginning, because it takes time for them all to work their way to the surface. But the field is fruitful every year, nonetheless. It can bear more and more fruit as the years go by and as the soil becomes more and more deeply cultivated and rock-free, but the fruit of the harvest begins to come long before all the rocks are gone.

So it is with sin and holiness in the life of the Christian. The process of rooting out sin is ongoing; we live in time, and our sanctification takes place over time. There are sins that only a mature Christian can repent of, because only a mature Christian can notice them. Sensitivity to sin is something that grows and develops. To the immature person in Christ, sin feels normal. It is primarily obvious sins that such a person can identify and repent of. But as we mature in Christ, we become more aware of spiritual realities and of God's requirements. Our consciences become more and more tender with regard to sin, and we are enabled to repent of sins we may not even have been aware of earlier. But in the midst of this ongoing process, holiness, real holiness, can characterize our lives. We are formed more and more closely into the image of our Savior, Christ, and our lives are filled increasingly with the "fruits of righteousness" (Phil. 1:9–11) and with a love that is both knowledgeable and discerning concerning God and God's will for our lives.

The result of the process of sanctification is a many-splendored holiness, as the range of God's desires for human wholeness shows forth in the lives of those who are in Christ. Holiness is not a straitjacket that forces diverse individuals into a single mold. Holiness is what frees us from the numbing, repetitive sameness of evil, and enables us to grow into the specific individuals and communities God means for us to be. So much of sin is divisive and isolating: jealousy, anger, envy, hatred, slander all fracture the relationships that are intrinsic to the kind of humanity for which God created us. In contrast, scripture uses words like compassion, kindness, humility, meekness, patience, forgiveness, gentleness, and peace to describe the holiness that God by his Holy Spirit works in the lives of Christians. These are relational words, and as such they are open to infinite variety: there are as many ways of being kind as there are persons who are kind and persons to be kind to.

The relational qualities of holy living are an indication of the intrinsically communal nature of Christian holiness. We all require both the guidance and the encouragement of others as we seek to repent of our sins and to increase in holiness. Holiness itself cannot be practiced apart from relationships with other people, both our fellow Christians and those who have not yet responded to the gospel. And even to know what holiness is, we need the shared wisdom of the Christian community, both of our own day and of past ages. It takes time, and the wisdom of generations, to come to understand the overarching Christian story and the way individual bits of the Bible fit into that story and inform the story of each of our lives. We therefore need to take care not to forget the insights of earlier generations of Christians. There are many things about the Christian life that they can teach us and that may aid us in discerning the specific content of holiness in our own day and time.

II

Sexual ethics is one particular dimension of a larger Christian ethic of holiness. For men and women alike, sexuality is a basic and far-reaching aspect of who we are. It should be no surprise to us, therefore, that the God who wishes for us to be renewed and conformed to his image at every level of our being should care deeply about our sexuality and our sexual conduct. We are called to set apart our sexuality for the purposes of God, and not to use it in the service of goals or desires that are contrary to the purposes of God. Christians have long been persuaded that the foundation of such sexual holiness is the dedication of all sexual activity to marriage.

Christians believe that God's creation of humans as male and female indicates that the sexual complementarity between men and women is one of the most basic ways in which God has structured human relationships. This complementarity between men and women finds its most specific and intimate expression in the coming together of one man and one woman in the covenant of marriage, a union that includes sexual relations. Sexual relations are thus a sign of the unity of husband and wife in the covenant of marriage. As husband and wife give themselves to each other sexually, they affirm their covenantal union, and the children who are the natural result of sex mark the fruitfulness that God intends for that union. The sexual complementarity of husband and wife and the a priori biological necessity of that complementarity for the children who are meant to be the fruit of marriage are why Christians have always understood marriage as inherently a covenant that unites a man and a woman. Marriage, sex, and children are related, in a Christian understanding, not externally or accidentally, but inherently and intentionally.

Christians have accordingly understood sex to be misused when it is exercised in ways that are opposed or alien to marriage and childbearing. These misuses of sex include adultery (sex that violates one's own or someone else's marriage vows), fornication (sex between unmarried persons), incest (sex with one's relatives), homosexual relations (sex with persons of one's own sex), promiscuity (sex with everybody and anybody), masturbation (sex all by oneself), pornography (sex by proxy), prostitution (sex for money), and bestiality (sex with animals). Christians do not believe that all of these acts are equally immoral, but they do believe that none of them is in accordance with God's creative and redemptive intentions for human sexuality. These acts are believed to be immoral not simply because there are biblical texts that forbid them—indeed, while some of these acts are forbidden in scripture, some are not mentioned at all. Christians believe these acts to be immoral because they believe such acts to be incompatible with chastity, the holy exercise of sexuality in both singleness and marriage, to which God calls all persons in Christ.

In the broadest sense, chastity is that sexual purity to which God calls each of us, whether single or married. In a narrower sense, the word *chastity* is sometimes used to refer specifically to sexual purity in singleness, while *fidelity* is used to refer to sexual purity in marriage. It is important to note that when the word *chastity* is used in its broader sense, it does not exclude sexual activity. Sexual relations in and of themselves do not make a person unchaste. The virgin, the widow and the widower, the divorced person, and the married person may all be equally chaste, as each seeks to live a life of sexual purity in either the married or the single state. For the unmarried person, chastity requires abstention from sexual relations. For the married person, chastity requires sexual fidelity to one's spouse. In addition, sex within marriage is to serve the purposes for which God intends it. These include the endearment of spouses to one another, the licit expression of sexual desire, and the procreation of children. If, on the other hand, one has sex with one's spouse with no interest in anything but one's own pleasure, this is hardly better than consorting with a prostitute.

Accordingly, we find throughout scripture exhortations and images which are meant to aid us in understanding aright both marriage and sexual behavior. Marriage is presented as the proper, God-given context for sexual relations. "Let marriage be held in honor among all," urges the author of the letter to the Hebrews (Heb. 13:4, RSV). We are to honor our own marriages by being faithful to our spouses, to honor other people's marriages by not committing adultery with other people's spouses, and to honor marriage itself by living out our own sexuality in a way that is chaste, whatever our marital status. Conversely, scripture associates sexual sin with idolatry. The prophets of the Old

Testament routinely describe Israel's sexual immorality as idolatry and her apostasy as adultery (Jer. 2:20–25; Ezek. 16:15ff.). In fact, what you do with your body shows whom you worship. A believer's body is a temple of the Holy Spirit, says Paul, and immoral sexual relations defile that temple (Rom. 6:18). Christians are thus to honor God with their bodies (1 Cor. 6:12–20), and to present their bodies as living sacrifices to God (Rom. 12:1).

Scriptural authors harbor no illusions that Christian people will necessarily have been living in a sexually pure manner all their lives. "Do not be deceived," says Paul; "neither the immoral, nor idolaters, nor adulterers, nor sexual perverts, nor thieves, nor the greedy, nor drunkards, nor revilers, nor robbers will inherit the kingdom of God. *And such were some of you.* But you were washed, you were sanctified, you were justified in the name of the Lord Jesus Christ and in the Spirit of our God" (1 Cor. 6:9–11, RSV, italics added). Sexual immorality, like other kinds of immorality, is very common. It is also incompatible with Christian holiness. Christians are called to put it behind them and to live the kind of sexually pure lives that are compatible with the gospel of Christ. Thus Jesus himself, in rescuing the woman taken in adultery from her self-appointed executioners, forgave her with the warning, "Go, and do not sin again" (John 8:3–11).

We who live in the Western culture of today often find it difficult to hear God's call to sexual holiness and to repentance from sexual sin. This is no doubt in part due to the sex-saturated nature of our culture and to the common belief that a mature and fulfilled person is a sexually active person, while a chaste person—particularly a chaste single person—is immature and unfulfilled at best and pathologically repressed at worst. The traditional Christian conviction that sex is for marriage and only for marriage thus looks at least quaint, and possibly repressive and damaging. As a result, some have been tempted to redefine what makes sex morally good and to change the criterion from marriage to something else, with the aim of making sexual activity morally good for unmarried persons as well as for those who are married.

Sometimes the suggested criterion is "responsibility." Morally good sex is sex that is responsible. What "responsible" usually means is that no one gets pregnant, no one gets a disease, and no one gets hurt. This kind of sexual morality is most often promoted in public forums, but sometimes Christian parents are tempted to teach it to their children, apparently in the hope that even if those children become sexually active, they will act in ways that do not hurt them. This criterion can also be used as a rationalization for things like the use of pornography, with the idea that "no one is getting hurt, so it must be all right." But there is no such thing as unchastity that does not hurt anybody. Either our exercise of sexuality brings us into closer conformity to God's character, or it hampers and destroys that conformity. We are damaged when we engage in sexual behavior that is contrary to God's call to chastity, and we are healed and sanctified as we allow God to shape our sexuality in ways that are pleasing to him.

Another suggested criterion for morally acceptable sex is "loving commitment." Morally good sex is sex that takes place within a loving, committed relationship. Sometimes it is specified that the relationship must be "monogamous," which makes it sound as if the envisioned relationship has something to do with marriage. But in fact, the phrase "monogamous committed relationship" is most commonly used to extend morally acceptable sex *beyond* marriage, not to restrict it *to* marriage. If a relationship between two persons is sufficiently loving and committed, then, it is suggested, sex within that relationship should be understood as morally good. This criterion is advanced most often in support of homosexual relations and in support of heterosexual relations between the unmarried. It goes unspoken that some relationships are generally not in view here. Relationships with one's parents or one's pets, no matter how loving or committed those relationships may be, are not usually considered licit contexts for sexual relations. Neither is even the most loving and committed relationship between two persons who are married but not to each other.

In fact, very often the criterion of "loving commitment" is

advanced by those who are persuaded that things like adultery and incest are always immoral, but fornication and homosexual relations can be morally good if pursued in a properly loving and committed way. Thus, while a traditional Christian sexual ethic considers all nonmarital sexual conduct to be contrary to God's purposes for human sexuality, the ethic of "loving commitment" considers only some of such conduct to be contrary to God's purposes. There is still a line drawn between morally acceptable and morally unacceptable conduct; the line is simply drawn in a different place. Traditional Christian ethics, following Christian scripture, draws the line between sex within marriage and sex that is not within marriage. The ethic of loving commitment draws the line between sex within certain kinds of loving relationships (not necessarily marital) and sex in other (unspecified) relationships, however loving they may be. But if the criterion for morally good sex is loving commitment, why should any loving and committed relationship exclude sexual relations? If the biblical distinction between marital and nonmarital sex is deemed irrelevant for distinguishing between sex that is morally acceptable and sex that is morally unacceptable, it is difficult to see why sex between parents and children, or brothers and sisters, or large groups of loving and committed friends should be considered morally wrong.

There is, however, an important distinction to be made between loving and committed relationships generally and marriage in particular. Christians are called to loving and committed relationships with a wide range of persons. Marriage, on the other hand, is a specific and unique relationship that forms the specific and unique context within which sexual relations are appropriate. Indeed, sexual relations are integral to marriage. One of the things that makes the marital relationship different from any other human relationship is that marriage is a covenant that is sealed by the sexual union of the participants. This unique intimacy between husband and wife is surely part of the reason why scripture portrays the union between God and his people in specifically marital terms. God does not just have a committed, loving relationship with his people. Christ is our bridegroom, and we are his bride. One of the ways in which we present ourselves as a pure and virginal bride to Christ is to live out our sexual lives in ways that are increasingly renewed and purified.

That Christians, both married and single, are called to live out their sexuality in chastity does not mean that such sexual purity comes naturally to all of us. In fact, it does not come naturally to any of us. We are all born broken into a broken world, and our "natural" inclinations are all too often expressions of our alienation from God, rather than of the Christlikeness into which God wishes to draw us. This is as true of our sexuality as it is of any other aspect of our being. Evolutionary psychologists suggest that having many sexual partners is natural for humans, and particularly for men; yet in the gospel God calls to chastity even the most naturally promiscuous of us. Similarly, homosexual orientation may be natural for some, yet God's call to chastity extends to homosexual persons as it does to all others. We cannot know the call of God in our lives simply by considering what seems "natural." We need rather to heed God's call to holiness, which is, after all, a call from sin to righteousness, from darkness to light, from idolatry to the right worship of the true God. To a fallen person, sexual holiness may seem profoundly unnatural; but to the person who is growing in grace, as he or she is renewed from within by the Holy Spirit, sexual holiness seems increasingly natural and increasingly desirable and delightful.

The degree to which each of us experiences a renewed sexuality and is enabled to live out a sexual life that is obedient to God may vary considerably. We are all equally sinners before God, but the damage that sin has done to us may differ in its specifics. Some people may struggle all their lives with anger or covetousness, but find it relatively easy to remain sexually pure. Others may find that sexual sin of one kind or another is a constant temptation. In fact, most of us are more susceptible to sexual sin than we would like to think, as the proliferation of pornography on the Internet sadly indicates. What sexual sins might we all fall into, if access to them were as easy as this? But most of us tend to suppose that the serious sexual sins are the ones other people are doing and that as long as we avoid doing those things, we are fine. We all need to be reminded that sexual purity, like any kind of holiness, is not a matter of keeping one's list of sins short and private and declaiming against those whose lists are longer or more public. Holiness is a positive quality, not a negative one, and there is always room for growth in holiness, always room for us to be more deeply renewed by the Holy Spirit and conformed to the likeness of Christ.

The Christian community needs to be a place where sexual holiness is fostered, where men and women encourage one another to strive after a rightly ordered sexuality, where confession of and repentance from sexual sin is routinely and compassionately received, where fidelity within the covenant of marriage and chastity in singleness are the standard of holiness to which all individually and together are encouraged and expected to aspire. The degree to which these things are true of the church may be the degree to which the church looks odd when measured by the norm of the surrounding culture. But the standard against which Christians are called be measured is the standard of God's holiness, of Christ's character, of the Holy Spirit's purity and power. May we in all things be so renewed that we may finally stand in the presence of God and behold his glory face to face.

Christian Vocation

Joseph B. Rightmyer

I n preceding chapters the reader has been given biblical and theological perspectives on the gracious vocation of Christ in our behalf. God through Christ has done something unique, of which we are the beneficiaries. Given that the work of creation and redemption is a fait accompli, and furthermore that all things present and future are complete in Christ Jesus, is there something we are to do in return? Do we have a vocation *toward* Christ? The revelation of scripture gives a resounding yes, accompanied by the further good news that the One who demands a response is also the One who effects the same! This is how our union with Christ leads us toward a joyous embrace of Christian vocation.

Applying the doctrine of union with Christ in the realm of Christian vocation has been a major theme of Reformation thought. By virtue of being partakers of the divine nature, believers are led toward an understanding of vocation that embraces obedient discipleship in every sphere of life. Work and worship, public and private activities, recreation and rest all are to reflect the glory of the One who has called us and united us to himself. Such is the broad scope of our vocation and calling in Christ. However, due to traditional and cultural definitions of vocation, focused attention will also be given to responding to Christ in the arena of employment and work, especially since jobs dominate so much of the American context. Learning to see our work as a calling given and directed by God becomes a vocation in and of itself, as demonstrated by Christ's own vigilance in prayer. In Christ's example and teaching, the believer is exhorted to do the work of guarding the heart and keeping open lines of communication with the Father. Through such processes of prayer and discernment, however, the Spirit also leads believers to the recognition when their work is done that it has been Christ at work in and through us all along!

Christ, through his ongoing and unique vocation as Lord, provides the basis and power for our calling as the Holy Spirit unites us with him. This willingness on the part of Christ to include human beings in the divine image *and* work is not only all-encompassing, but also very particular and personal. In Christ, our motivations and actions as disciples take on a shape that is radically different from those that our culture recognizes and understands. Grounded in a perspective that the world around us can neither see nor understand, we pursue our life's calling in faith, knowing what Christ has completed in himself and what he has chosen to complete in us. The remarkable truth is that he has chosen to include us in his work. This recognition prevents us from developing an arrogant and false sense of self-sufficiency on the one hand, and becoming paralyzed and fearful on the other.

In a very real sense, every time a person is asked, "What in the world are you doing?" the answer should reflect the very activity of Christ in and through each believer. Christ grants an intimate awareness of his presence in the lives of each of his disciples. His expressed purpose in doing so is to channel the life-giving and fruit-bearing Spirit through human beings as vessels so that disciples may share in the life, joy, and glory of Christ himself. In the same passage in which Jesus declares that our purpose is to bear fruit, he also promises to provide whatever is needed to accomplish the task (John 15:16). This is the true nature of Christian discipleship and vocation. We are not given responsibilities and then sent out to make it all happen somehow by our own strength. Rather, we are the vessels through whom Christ has chosen to do his work.

Such an understanding of our vocation is consistent with the calling of Christ himself in relationship with his Father. In John 8:28–29 (NASB), the remarkable identity of Christ and his faithful obedience is revealed when he says, "I do nothing on My own initiative, but I speak these things as the Father taught Me. And He who sent Me is with Me; He has not left Me alone, for I always do the things that are pleasing to Him."

This and other passages in the gospels make it abundantly clear that Jesus lived his earthly life in such constant fellowship with his Father that his every thought, word, and deed were in loving accord with the will of the One who sent him. He knew precisely what he was called to do. He had a vocation that encompassed every action, every conversation, and every miracle he undertook. Such a life was not programmed in the sense that he had no responsibility and will. His earthly identification with us in the flesh meant that he had to study, to pray, to resist temptation, and to die. He, being tempted in every way that we are (Heb. 4:15), approached life through meditation upon scripture (Luke 2:52) and attention to prayer (Luke 11:1). We are instructed to do the same.

Such a manner of life was not only instructive, but also productive, for through this communion with the Father he both understood and performed the radical, costly obedience of offering himself as a sacrifice for sin and for the salvation of the world. Everything in heaven and earth has been reconciled in Christ to the Father and ultimately will redound to the glory of God. In order to accomplish this purpose, Christ had to overcome the shortsighted "wisdom" of those who would discourage him from his vocation, including the disciples. His was a calling that emanated from the One who had sent him, who had promised a fruitful future, even beyond death and the grave. Because of this intimacy with the Father and the indwelling presence of the Holy Spirit during his sojourn, he was obedient even unto death. Therefore God has highly exalted him and given him the name that is above every other name in heaven and on earth. Christ's obedient response to God's will in the power of the Holy Spirit is forever vindicated by his resurrected and ascended Lordship.

No higher honor can be given. No greater obedience can be offered. The Father has given the highest and the best to the Son, for the Son is worthy. He stands alone in his redemptive, reconciling vocation. For this reason we bow before him, offering honor and praise and glory for ever and ever! He is Lord and King.

Therefore, his vocation is unique and demands a response. What are we to do in light of such a vocation of Christ in our behalf? How do we respond? What is our vocation toward him?

Interestingly enough, the apostle Paul anticipates our question, for immediately following the affirmation of Jesus' authoritative stature in his letter to the Philippians, he summarizes our vocation in words that both give us our commands and inform us of the power to do them: "So then, my beloved, just as you have always obeyed . . . work out your salvation with fear and trembling; for it is God who is at work in you, both to will and to work for His good pleasure" (Phil. 2:12–13, NASB).

Union with Christ:
The Basis for Vocation as Discipleship

The New Testament is replete with exhortations to live for Christ in all of life. We are called to be disciples. That is our vocation. But the task is impossible part from our union with Christ. The strong declaration of the apostle Peter regarding his devotion to Christ, followed by his denials and display of spiritual impotence, are highly instructive here.

Peter wanted to serve Christ. We have every reason to believe that when he made his fateful declaration, "I will *not* deny you!" (Mark 14:31), he had every intention of keeping his promise. His life had been touched by the three years spent in discipleship training with his Master. He truly believed that Jesus was the Christ, the Son of the living God, and he wanted to love and serve Jesus in turn.

Many a saint has made the same declaration. When the Holy Spirit makes personally present the saving action of Jesus Christ in the life of a particular believer, there is a natural and grateful response that wells up from within the soul. Many believers, especially following a momentous insight or ecstasy in worship, have pledged undivided loyalty and a willingness to serve Christ anywhere in the world. Such sentiment is real and sincere. The problem lies in a misunderstanding of our spiritual nature and an overestimation of our human will.

Even the apostle Peter had to learn the lesson about the difference between human will and divine nature. Peter had been gifted with unparalleled insight about the person of Jesus and exclaimed accurately, "You are the Christ, the Son of the living God." To this Jesus replied, "Flesh and blood has not revealed this to you, but my Father in heaven" (Matt. 16:16–17, NRSV). It was Peter's discovery, but it was not because of Peter's intellect. It was a momentous occasion of faith when the spirit of Peter connected with the Spirit of Christ in recognition of who was at work in the earth. Therefore, Christ affirmed Peter in his confession and declared that this apostle holding this perspective about Jesus would be the foundation of the church. The Master can build upon affirmations of faith that are centered in a clear of understanding of the True Worker of God's will.

The Master, however, does not build upon false affirmations. Therefore, when Peter announced complete loyalty based upon human resolve, Christ contradicted him. In a conversation that apparently lasted only a few minutes Peter was introduced to the complete Lordship of Christ. In Peter's self-affirmation, "I will not deny you," Christ perceived willful, prideful, and even satanic motivations emanating from sinful flesh. Therefore, Jesus rebuked Peter for his faulty view of self, setting the scene for Peter's painful discovery that his own strength would fail him, that he would deny Christ three times before daybreak despite all his good intentions (Luke 22:31–34). However, true to his own character and vocation, Christ went on to declare the truth about his own sufficiency, announcing to Peter that he, Jesus, would intercede for him and, in God's good time, would give him the Spirit to effect success in his vocation as a disciple. Christ thus proved himself faithful despite Peter's faithlessness.

Can it be that Jesus Christ gives love, joy, peace, patience, goodness, kindness, gentleness, faithfulness, and self-control to every individual who believes? Can we add to that list wisdom, knowledge, understanding, and power? Is there anything that we need that Christ has not promised to provide? One of the great paradoxes of the Christian faith is that Jesus demands faithful obedience from his disciples, but instead of expecting us to produce the results by our own will or strength, Christ produces the fruit within us. Herein lies the great truth about our union with Christ as it affects our vocation. Christ both calls us to service and enables the ministry of the same calling. Christ in us is not only the hope of glory, but is also the source of life throughout our earthly sojourn. It is precisely in this context that we more fully understand that "it is God who is at work within you, both to will and to do his good pleasure" (Phil. 2:13, KJV alt.).

If Christ is indeed at work within us, which areas of our lives will feel the effects? Within what relationships and tasks of life will Jesus bring his truth to bear? The astounding answer is, every single one! Christ's Lordship establishes the reign of God over everything by the power of the Holy Spirit. As affirmed in "Union with Christ: A Declaration for the Church," "Jesus is . . . the truly human one. His coming transforms everything."[1] This means that the reign of God in Jesus Christ affects our public life as well as our private, our work as well as our worship. It eliminates any false distinctions between sacred and secular, giving value and worth to each act of kindness and every form of legitimate business as well as commonly understood "church vocations." It establishes us in the awareness of our calling as disciples in front of our computers as well as in church chancels. Jesus calls and empowers us as his ambassadors in board meetings as well as session meetings. He has a word about how we treat the trash collector as well as the deacon holding the offering plate. The reign of God often calls us to do the trash collecting, and to do it to the glory of God. Vocationally, our union with Christ provides an answer to the question, "What in the world is

God doing?" Christ affirms that his reign, his life in us, makes the activity of God and the vocation of believers one and the same.

The scope of application of our union with Christ in reference to our activities is as broad as life itself. Our union with Christ is so complete, so exhaustive, that everything we do should be a reflection of Christ's heart and mind. It is in this context that Paul exhorted the church in Colossae: "And whatever you do in word or deed, do all in the name of the Lord Jesus, giving thanks through Him to God the Father" (Col. 3:17, NASB). In rapid order Paul identifies categories of activity encompassed under the rubric of "all things," listing marriage, parenting, service to others, running a business, conduct toward unbelievers, and speaking. This is the intent of the summary of "Christian Vocation" in the Directory for Worship of the Presbyterian Church (U.S.A.), which reads:

> God calls a people to believe in Jesus Christ as Lord and Savior; to follow Jesus Christ in obedient discipleship; to use gifts and abilities God has given, honoring and serving God in personal life, in households and in families, in daily occupation, in community, nation, and the world.
> . . . Persons respond to God's call to honor and serve God in every aspect of human life, in their work and in their play, in their thought and in their action, in their private and in their public relationships. God hallows daily life, and daily life provides opportunity for holy living. As Christians honor and serve God in daily life, they worship God. For Christians, work and worship cannot be separated.[2]

As Presbyterians we affirm this understanding of Christian vocation. By virtue of our union with Christ, the affirmation is not only a statement, but also a living demonstration of the presence of Christ to will and enable his high calling in us and in every sphere of our lives.

Union with Christ: The Basis for Vocation as Work

While it is important to understand the all-encompassing nature of Christian vocation, it is instructive also to narrow the focus and examine the theme in relation to employment or work, given that jobs command so much time, thought, and energy in the surrounding culture. Vocation in the North American context typically refers to an occupation, business, profession, or trade. We often view such "work" not only as the means by which we earn an income, but also as the factor by which we measure our social status or self-worth. A particular job often dominates our decisions about where or how we will live; it becomes a source of tension between competing individuals or spouses and often creates enormous stress. The enormous influence of work in our lives underscores our need for a perspective on work that is grounded in an understanding of our union with Christ.

Our occupational vocation takes on a completely different meaning in light of our union with Christ. For believers, the good news about the kingdom ushers us into new understandings of work as well. Through Christ we come to see our work as involving the activity of Christ as much as what we do. Therefore, our vocation or calling when understood in the context of our union with Christ, is the activity of none other than Christ in and through us by the power of the Holy Spirit. This definition teaches us that Christ himself gives significance to what we do and calls us to our work with a different understanding of its purpose and fulfillment.

While there are particular vocations—such as apostles, evangelists, prophets, and pastor-teachers—that are unique to the body of Christ and provide distinct leadership in the community of faith, union with Christ affects all types of vocations as work, both inside and outside the church. For a Christian, the important contrast is not the commonly held distinction between sacred and secular occupations, but the contrast between views of work that reflect Christ and those that reflect the values of secular culture.

Our culture often looks upon work as a necessary evil by means of which we can improve our standard of living and enjoy increased comfort. Pressure is being applied to shorten the work week in order to increase leisure time. Our culture further sees retirement as the reward for years of labor, the occasion when one has enough accumulated wealth so that work is no longer necessary. Work is something we seek to avoid, rather than being something inherently fulfilling.

The creation story teaches us that such has not always been the case. In fact, a careful study of the Scriptures provides insight into the fact that God is the original worker and that we, being created in the image of God, are to experience work as re-creative and fulfilling. The joy of exploration and discovery, of identifying and naming the animals, and of having dominion over the rest of creation was a gift from God in order that humankind might delight in being participants in the vocation of God.

It is instructive to know what God was doing prior to creation, in order more fully to understand how creativity and work reflect our being created in God's image. John 17:24 reveals that the Father loved the Son even before the foundation of the earth. Ephesians 1:3–14 uses several expressions to speak of "choosing before the creation of the world," of "predestination and adoption," and of planning to fulfill the divine mystery through the foreordained ministry of Jesus Christ. It is clear that the persons of the Godhead—Father, Son, and Holy Spirit—shared love, thought, and communication. There was intimacy. There was planning and designing. There were decisions. There was action.

The action, proceeding from the motive of overflowing love and enabled by a self-sufficient power to create out of nothing, revealed the desire on the part of God to share life and glory with a world and its inhabitants in a manner consistent with the very image of God. Therefore, the love, thought, and communication that marked the Persons of the Trinity prior to creation became the characteristics of humanity in the image of God *following* creation. Even though the plan appeared to be thwarted by the introduction of sin through the willful disobedience of Adam and Eve, the reality is that in Jesus Christ, by the power of the Holy Spirit, the purposes of God the Father would be fulfilled according to a predetermined plan to reconcile all things to God.

Mistaken interpretations of Genesis 3 can lead to the belief that work is part of the curse upon humankind as a result of the Fall. However, a close inspection of Gen. 3:17–19 will reveal that it was the ground that was cursed, not work itself. Certainly the introduction of sin into the world had an impact on work. Weeds entered the scene, adding toil to the task of caring for the garden. Dominion became entangled with "thorns and thistles." Childbirth became intensely painful. Individuals who had lived in mutual trust became the objects of blame and violence. Community life degenerated into contests of power politics. Vocations, especially in the sense of daily work, began to be seen as activities to be avoided rather than enjoyed. The consequences and misunderstandings resulting from that original sin continue to this very day.

Recovery of the truth about work and its intended joy and fulfillment can begin with a fresh look at the biblical story of creation, with God seen as the original worker. In a very real sense, the vocation of God (creating, redeeming, and sustaining life) is reflected in the work of creation. In turn, our vocations reflect the very image of God, who, through Christ, planned, designed, engineered, developed, managed, and produced a creation that was good. It was completed work, for at the end of the days of creation God rested. The work of God was very creative and fulfilling. It had a purpose consistent with the character of God. Prior to creation, the Persons of the Trinity consulted with one another, planned the entire work from creation to consummation, and executed the same in and through Christ Jesus.

God called Adam and Eve to tend and care for the garden as gracious invitation to share in the image of God, that image being here reflected in activity and work. It was the choice of God to share with created beings the unfolding drama of life on earth. For sure, there is a distinct difference between the kind of work that God accomplished and the work that is given human beings to do. God created out of nothing, demonstrating the prerogative and power that distinguishes God as God. Our work can only handle and shape what God has already created, the stuff and matter of earth. This difference notwithstanding, it is still given to human beings to experience and reflect the image of God by working, and to see labor as a good thing.

In this first economy, the work of Adam was not drudgery, but

fulfillment and satisfaction. And the broader context of vocation—discipleship in every activity—reflects God's gracious calling to bear the divine image and to delight in God's good gifts.
God called the man and the woman to reflect and rejoice in the
image of their Creator not only by their work, but also in their
loving communion with one another, with the offspring of their
relationship, and eventually with a broader community. God
establishes the vocation of each individual and also of the corporate community with the intent that humanity should experience
abundant and joyous living—forever!

It is noteworthy that Adam was not placed in the garden and
abandoned. God sought him for fellowship and participation in
the divine image and activity. It was the desire of God to be in
constant relationship—union, if you will—in such a way that
everything Adam did, vocationally and relationally, would be
directly affected by the wisdom and power of the One who had
designed him. The proper vocation of Adam toward God was a
response of trust, marked by obedience to the divine plan in
every area of life. God intended life in such union to be exciting
and exhilarating. Adam was not programmed like a robot in such
a way that faithfulness and obedience in vocations and relationships would be mindless. Rather, God gave Adam the opportunity to live as a king in the sense of Solomon when he penned,
"It is the glory of God to conceal a matter, but the glory of kings
is to search out a matter" (Prov. 25:2, NASB). Surely this was what
God had in mind when he said to Adam, "From any tree of the
garden you may eat freely." It was an invitation to explore the
dimensions of his calling: to investigate, to think, to plumb the
depths of God's creation. It is the basis of joy for anyone who
participates in any of the arts and sciences. To compose a piece
of music or to build a bridge is the source of immense satisfaction to the one who has studied and applied the laws at work in
each discipline. And that is what God intended, for the "laws of
nature" are in reality the laws of God, established for our good
and part of the created order that provides the framework for
our participation in the ongoing, sustaining vocation of Christ.

God's intentions still stand. In faith believers can still understand and receive the wondrous thrill of being partakers of the divine nature, seeing and experiencing life in a dimension that the world will never know. Every activity becomes an opportunity for discipleship. The meaning and purpose of work is restored, as well as the joy of learning and discovery. Success in terms of the kingdom, not in terms of the culture, is guaranteed, for the call to vocation in Christ is dependent not upon the strength of human will, but the presence and power of Christ in us by the Holy Spirit. This is part of what it means to be created in the image of God, with the Son faithful to the Father. Because of the faithfulness of Christ, we can be faithful. Christ works in us and through us for his own glory. This indeed is the heart of how our union with Christ undergirds our vocation, our life's calling.

NOTES

1. "Union with Christ: A Declaration for the Church," Presbyterian Coalition, 1998.
2. *Book of Order* (Louisville, Ky.: Presbyterian Church [U.S.A.] 1999), W-5.6000–5.6003.

Dying to Live

Romans 6:1–14

Peter B. Barnes

Larry Walters is a thirty-three-year-old truck driver whose boyhood dream was to fly. When he graduated from high school, he joined the Air Force in hopes of becoming a pilot. Unfortunately, poor eyesight disqualified him. When he was finally discharged, he had to satisfy himself watching jets fly over his backyard in southern California—until he took matters into his own hands. He used forty-two six-foot diameter weather balloons that he purchased from a local army surplus store, tied them with a fifty-foot cable to a Sears lawnchair and pumped them full of helium. Six friends set the craft loose (which he had fondly dubbed "Inspiration I") from the jeep he used to hold it on the ground. Larry was airborne.

His plan to was rise to about a hundred feet, but everything didn't go as planned when the tethers broke. Minutes later, Larry was frantically calling for help over his citizens band radio. It seems that the lawn chair soared up to sixteen thousand feet (that's right, three miles!) and entered into the airspace of the Los Angeles airport. Larry really "lost his grip" when his freezing fingers caused him to accidentally drop both a BB pistol (to shoot the balloons when he wanted to descend) and his CB radio. The lawn chair drifted downward, loosely controlled as he jettisoned the gallon jugs of water attached to the sides of the chair as ballast. As he neared the ground, he spotted power lines, but the balloons fortunately draped themselves across the wires and left Larry comfortably in his chair about five feet from the ground. He finished what was left of his soda and jumped back to earth. The crash landing knocked out power in the Long Beach area for twenty minutes.

The stunt, in 1997, earned Walters the Darwin Award, the top prize given by the Bonehead Club of Dallas. He also had to pay a $1,500 fine to the FAA for operating a civil aircraft for which there was not an airworthiness certificate.[1]

There are times in our lives when we find ourselves in a bad situation, and we make further bad decisions that only make it worse. That is as true in spiritual matters as in trying to fly in a lawn chair. Paul writes about this in Romans 6.

In explicating the gospel to the believers in Rome, the apostle answers the objection that the doctrine of justification by faith logically leads to more sin in a person's life. The objection goes something like this: "If all my sins have already been paid for, if living a moral life can't save me, then why should I even try to be good? Why not go out and sin all I want, because Christ is going to forgive the Christian's sin anyway?" The problem with this way of thinking, which is called antinomianism, is that this kind of living only compounds the problem. The further bad decisions only complicate the already bad situation.

To the question, "Shall we go on sinning that grace may increase?" Paul responds bluntly in verse 2, "By no means!"— "No way! God forbid! Not on your life!"—and he goes on to explain why. The very idea of willfully living in sin with the notion that we are somehow inviting more of God's grace should be unthinkable for the Christians; it makes a mockery of God's love and grace and our calling to be his faithful disciples. Paul says that a true follower of Jesus Christ cannot continue to live in sin without sensing his or her own guilt and conviction before God and desiring to turn from it.

There is a subtle temptation we all experience from time to time in our own lives that says, "Go ahead. Everyone's doing it.

No one will ever know. Besides, God will forgive you anyway." Paul uses three verbs to counter this temptation: know, consider, and offer. Let's consider each of these briefly.

Know That You Have Been Joined with Christ

In verses 3–10 Paul writes the words "Don't you know," or "For we know" three times, and the statements he makes can be summarized by the affirmation, "Know that you have been joined with Christ." He reminds us that as Christians we have been baptized. Being baptized as a Christian involves a personal identification with Jesus. It marks our inclusion into the covenant community of faith. And our baptism, Paul says, has been a baptism into Christ's death and resurrection. What happened to Christ physically has happened to us spiritually, in that through our baptism we die to the old life and are raised to a new life in Christ.

In the medieval church, when a monk joined a Benedictine monastery, he actually came and lay down at the front of the church, right where the body would lie at the time of a funeral. They literally put a funeral pall over the person and rang the bells to signify that someone had died. Then there was a long period of silence. That silence was wonderfully interrupted by a song from the book of Colossians that says, "For you have died and your life is hid with Christ and God." After a little more silence, the monks began singing from Psalm 118, "I shall not die but live and declare the words of the Lord." After one more period of silence, they broke into spontaneous words of triumph from 1 Corinthians: "Awake, O sleeper, and arise from the dead, and Christ will shine on you!" The bells of the abbey started to ring, and the new brother was embraced into this new order. Becoming a Christian is very much like dying to one way of life and rising to another. That is what the old baptismal liturgy meant. It meant going under the water to an old way of life and rising again to a new one.

In January of 1992 I had the great privilege of spending two weeks in India on a short-term mission trip. During that trip we visited the small rural village of Kotapata, where we witnessed a service of baptism. Twelve people were baptized that day, people of the village who had recently come to faith in Jesus Christ. They came out of Hinduism and Islam to a new and living faith in Jesus Christ. The service was public, out in the open, as a testimony to the townspeople as well as to the members of the church. We sang songs and paraded through the village as we walked out to the rice paddies. There the pastor asked those being baptized several questions, and he invited them to renounce evil in their lives and in the world. When each individual who was baptized came up out of the water, the pastor gave him or her a new name. For example, the pastor would say, "You are now Mary, a believer in Jesus Christ. May you be as the mother of our Lord, who was willing to be the handmaiden of God." Paul says in this passage in Romans that you and I have been joined to Christ in baptism; therefore, we must make a break with the past. I am a new person, and my identity is now in Christ.

Consider This to Be So

"In the same way, count yourselves dead to sin but alive to God in Christ Jesus. Therefore do not let sin reign in your mortal body so that you obey its evil desires" (Rom. 6:11–12, NIV).

What Paul is saying here is that we must make a decision to act in harmony with, and on the basis of, our new relationship with Christ. We must choose to put into practice the truth about ourselves regarding our lives in him. And when we are tempted to go back to our old ways of living, we must consider that the old person we used to be is now dead, and that the new person we are becoming in Christ is alive.

Philip Yancey relates that Harvard biologist Edward O. Wilson once performed a rather bizarre experiment on ants that sheds light on Paul's admonition in this passage. After noticing that it took ants a few days to recognize one of their crumpled nestmates as having died, Wilson determined that ants identified death by clues of smell, not sight. As the ant's body began to decompose, other ants would invariably carry it out of the nest to a refuse pile. After many attempts, Wilson narrowed down the chemical clue to oleic acid. If the ants smelled oleic acid, they would carry out the corpse; any other smell they ignored. Their instinct was so strong that if Wilson daubed oleic acid on bits of paper, other ants would dutifully carry the paper to the ant cemetery.

Wilson even painted oleic acid on the bodies of living ants, and sure enough, their nestmates seized and marched these living ants, their legs and antennae wriggling in protest, out to the ant cemetery. Left there, the indignant "living dead" cleaned themselves off before returning to the nest. If they did not remove every trace of the oleic acid, the other ants would promptly seize them again and return them to the cemetery.

This image of "dead" ants acting very much alive is what Paul is talking about in this passage. Sin may be dead, but it stubbornly wriggles back to life.[2] Or as Martin Luther is reputed to have said, "I tried to drown the old Adam in the waters of baptism, but the miserable wretch can swim!"

Paul writes, "Count yourselves dead to sin but alive to God in Christ Jesus" (Rom. 6:11, NIV). This considering, this reckoning is not make-believe. It is not screwing up our faith to believe in a myth. We are not to pretend that our old nature has gone away, when we know perfectly well it has not. Rather, we are to realize and remember that our former identity and life apart from God did die with Christ, and we put an end to its career. We are to consider what in fact we are: dead to sin and alive to God. When the subtle temptations come to go back to our old ways, we need to say, "That person doesn't live here anymore."

Offer Yourself to God

"Do not offer the parts of your body to sin, as instruments of wickedness, but rather offer yourselves to God, as those who have been brought from death to life; and offer the parts of your body to him as instruments of righteousness" (Rom. 6:13, NIV).

Here Paul calls us to offer ourselves and our bodies not to sin, but to God, and as a motive for such action, he appeals to the fact that we are now no longer under the reign of law but under grace.

Yancey writes, "Sin is a slave master that controls us whether we like it or not. Paradoxically, a headlong pursuit of freedom often turns into bondage: insist on the freedom to lose your temper whenever you feel anger, and you will soon find yourself a slave to rage. In modern life, those things that teenagers do to express their freedom—tobacco, alcohol, drugs, pornography—become their relentless masters."[3]

One of the paradoxes of the Christian faith is that in seeking freedom in Christ, we must submit ourselves to his rule. We exchange masters, as it were, and become slaves of Christ rather than slaves to sin, and therein lies our freedom. The novelist François Mauriac says it well: "This enslavement [to Christ] is really a miraculous liberation, for even when you were free you spent the whole time forging chains for yourself and putting them on, riveting them tighter and tighter each moment. During the years when you thought you were free you submitted like an ox to the yoke of your countless hereditary ills. From the hour of your birth not one of your crimes has failed to go on living, has failed to imprison you more and more every day, has failed to beget other crimes. The Man you submit yourself to does not want you to be free to be a slave: He breaks the circle of your fetters, and, against your half-extinguished and still-smoldering desires, He kindles and re-kindles the fire of Grace."[4]

Later on in chapter 12 of this letter, the apostle puts it this way, "Therefore, I urge you, brothers, in view of God's mercy, to offer your bodies as living sacrifices, holy and pleasing to God— this is your spiritual act of worship." (Rom. 12:1–2, NIV). A friend of mine once said to me, "You know, the problem with living sacrifices is that they keep climbing down off the altar!" Just when I think I have the thing settled with God and I seek to live for Him, there I go crawling down from my place of sacrifice and worship, and I find myself dealing with it all over again.

Instead of giving in to sin and letting it rule over our bodies, Paul suggests that we are to pursue a positive alternative—we are to offer ourselves to God. Our limbs, our organs, our eyes and ears and hands and feet, our minds, all that we are, our human faculties and capacities, our thoughts, our dreams—all are to be given over to God and his service. We should not hold anything back. No area of our lives should be withheld.

Are you willing to make that kind of commitment to Christ? The old African American spiritual says it well, "Give me Jesus, Give me Jesus. You can have all this world, just give me Jesus."

Conclusion

Know, consider, offer: These are the three verbs of dying in order to live. In writing about this passage, John Stott asks,

> Can a married woman live as though she were still single? Well, yes, I suppose she could. It is not impossible. But let her remember who she is. Let her feel her wedding ring, the symbol of her new life of union with her husband, and she will want to live accordingly. Can . . . Christians live as though they were still in their sins? Well, yes, I suppose they could, at least for a while. It is not impossible. But let them remember who they are. Let them recall their baptism, the symbol of their new life of union with Christ, and they will want to live accordingly. . . .
>
> Christians should no more contemplate a return to [the old way of] living than adults to their childhood, married people to their singleness or discharged prisoners to their prison cell. For our union with Jesus Christ has severed us from the old life and committed us to the new. Our baptism stands between the two like a door between two rooms, closing on the one and opening into the other.[5]

It is inconceivable that we should go back to our old way of living by willfully persisting in sin and presuming on God's grace. The very thought is a contradiction in terms. So we need constantly to remind ourselves who we are. We should ask ourselves, as did Paul, "Don't you know? Don't you know the meaning of your conversion and baptism? Don't you know that you have been united with Christ in his death and resurrection? Don't you know who you are?" And we should answer, "Yes, I do know who I am. I am a new person in Christ, and by the grace of God, I shall live accordingly."

On May 28, 1972, the Duke of Windsor, the former King Edward VIII, died in Paris. That same evening the news presented a retrospective of his life and showed extracts from earlier films and videos in which he answered questions about his upbringing, his brief reign, and his abdication of the throne in order to marry a commoner. Recalling his boyhood as the Prince of Wales, he said, "My father [King George V] was a strict disciplinarian. Sometimes when I had done something wrong, he would admonish me saying, 'My dear boy, you must always remember who you are.' "[6]

My friend, our heavenly Father says the same to you and me every day: "My dear child, you must remember who you are, and whose you are." We are sons and daughters of the King, saved by the blood of the Lamb, redeemed at the cost of his life, and in our baptism our old self died with Christ, and we were raised to a new life of possibility and hope. Don't go back to your old ways. Remember who you are . . . and whose you are. Amen.

NOTES

1. Adapted from accounts by United Press International, the Associated Press, and the Darwin Awards
2. Philip Yancey, *What's So Amazing about Grace?* (Grand Rapids: Zondervan Publishing House, 1997), 186, 187.
3. Ibid., 187.
4. François Mauriac, *God and Mammon* (London: Sheed & Ward, 1946), 68–69.
5. John R. W. Stott, *Romans* (Downers Grove, Ill.: InterVarsity Press, 1994), 179–80.
6. Adapted from Stott, *Romans*, 187–88.

One Life to Live

1 Kings 10:23–11:6 and Col. 2:6–7

Mary Holder Naegeli

King Solomon's life was a study in contradictions, some of which remain a mystery to us almost three thousand years after his reign in Israel. His rise to power began at the death of his father David, from whom he inherited a relatively stable nation. Solomon realized King David's dream by financing and constructing the Temple of the Lord, and it was a great day of celebration when the Ark of the Covenant was permanently installed in its final home.

His heartfelt wish as he felt the crushing weight of responsibility was for God to give him divine wisdom. Here was a man who knew his limitations! He went straight to the source of power and guidance—God Almighty, who had appeared to him in a dream—and requested not riches or prestige but the mind of God in practical matters. He wanted to be deeply rooted and built up spiritually for the awesome task of ruling the nation of Israel. Considering all the things Solomon could have asked for, God was impressed with his request and gave him much more besides: wealth and honor and a world-class reputation.

Over the next twenty years, Solomon amassed unbelievable wealth, forged international alliances by marriage to foreign women, built up an army, and constructed many fine buildings and fortified cities throughout Israel. He commanded a huge administrative staff that managed the day-to-day affairs of a vast and highly developed realm. Meanwhile, Solomon shared his wisdom with international visitors including the queen of Sheba. At the height of his influence, he was clearly one of the most prominent and popular monarchs in the world.

He was also under a lot of stress. Hundreds of officials looked to him for leadership in foreign trade, politics, and domestic economics. He made major decisions every day and was counted upon to offer God's wisdom to the whole world when asked. And after a hard day at work conducting the affairs of a growing country, you would expect him to retreat to his home for solitude, a quiet meal with his family, an hour of storytelling around the fire before retiring for the night. But even home was not a refuge! Just imagine the complications of managing a harem of seven hundred wives and three hundred concubines! Aside from the social pressures and the conjugal expectations, these women filled his palace court with their pagan gods. From one wing to another in the palace courts, the king of Israel would walk past idols of stone, wood, and metal, and his wives—whom he loved—sought his affirmation and acceptance. At work, in his public persona, he was God's man. At home, he embraced a pagan worldview. He successfully compartmentalized his life into segments with different masters.

When did Solomon cross the line? At what point did Solomon's political expediency evolve into personal, spiritual apostasy? During which conversation did Solomon's heart take steps toward the Sidonian Ashtoreth? Precisely when did the gracious provision of YHWH fade into the background and the insatiable needs of Molech take over? When was the tree of godly wisdom uprooted and cast off to decay in his inhospitable soul?

At what point did Solomon's heart divide? Was it in a moment of weakness as he was seduced by the attractive paganism of his favorite wife? Or was it in a moment of strength as he stepped in compassionately to make a newcomer to the palace court feel welcomed and accepted? The scriptures tell us that "as Solomon grew old, his wives turned his heart after other gods, and his heart was not fully devoted to the LORD his God" (1 Kings 11:4, NIV). Did Solomon get tired of fighting the spiritual battle for his soul? Or did he come to the conclusion, after all those years, that the path of wisdom was leading him to be more open-minded? At what point did the faith Solomon had been taught become irrelevant or untrue for him? When did it happen that he lost his gratitude for the stupendous success God had allowed him to enjoy?

Sadly, we do not know the moment, and we cannot identify the split second when his foot slipped on the path. It would be good for us to know this for our own instruction, since we too struggle to keep our faith and life in line with each other. What we do know is that Solomon's road differentiated itself from God's when he married that first pagan wife, contrary to God's explicit prohibition (Ex. 34:12–16). His path meandered in parallel for awhile, then gently explored the rolling hills of new experience, until it became obvious that Solomon and God were no longer in the same country.

We can appreciate the subtlety of Solomon's process as we try to balance the day-to-day affairs of contemporary American life. Juggling the various demands of faith, love, and work is very hard. The stresses in one area often send us looking for comforts provided by another. We find our Christian faith at odds with the values of the world, placing us in uncomfortable positions on the job or requiring subtle compromises of ethics along the way. We feel pulled in one direction by the faith that was taught us, but we feel our spiritual roots giving way when we cannot figure out how to apply those lessons at work. It is a symptom of our age that we have detached religious faith from our work, our politics, and our recreation. We Americans have taken the concept of "separation of church and state" to such a misguided extreme that we have created the impression that faith is now completely irrelevant to all human endeavor.

Let us say, for a moment, that this is true—that it is possible to separate our faith and our work into two different realms with no practical relationship. What are the options Christians employ to deal with this disconnection?[1]

Many Christians faithfully commute between these two worlds. The religious is relegated to Sunday mornings, and the secular takes over on Monday morning (or perhaps at noon on Sunday!). While I am at church, I am engaged in spiritual things that make sense and have truth in them, and I feel uplifted by the music and the fellowship as an added bonus. But then I commute to the world of work where another, completely different set of values prevails. I adopt those values out of expediency. "Whatever works" is what I do. The fact that my boss requires something of questionable ethics is subsumed under the heading of "company loyalty" or "profit at all cost." When I come home at night, I put all the ugliness of the day behind me and hug my spouse and children, watch my language, teach my kids the meaning of honesty, and otherwise revert to my privately held belief system. As an extreme illustration of this pattern, you recall the story of a German SS officer, who has overseen the killing of countless Jews that day, coming home for dinner with his wife and family and playing Mozart on the piano before going to bed. One life does not inform the other at all. For many of us, commuting from one world to the other is the practical reality of everyday life.

Another option Christians employ is to devalue the work "out there" as "just a job" or of no personal significance to me or to God. The tendency here is to place great value on the "spiritual" aspects of life, like going to church, teaching Sunday school, praying, and reading my Bible. This choice says that the work I do forty hours a week is of no lasting consequence and therefore irrelevant to my spiritual life and to God's will. I had a man tell me recently that his wife, who was the superintendent of their Sunday school, was doing the really important work of their family, while he was merely earning a living with his sales job. Though I appreciated the support and affirmation he gave to his wife in ministry, I was greatly saddened that he thought so little of the setting and the activity in which *he* was engaged!

The third option Christians employ is by their actions to devalue their faith and place far greater emphasis on the so-called secular aspects of life. More than ever, this resolution to the inner conflict seems justifiable, since companies have sought to play roles traditionally covered by the church. I can throw myself completely into my work when my employer fosters a sense of belonging, encourages community activism and altruism, and adopts core values that bring unity and effectiveness to the labor force. I can be lulled into an attractive, though incomplete, sense of purpose in such an environment. Who needs church if my workplace can do all that!

All three of these options—commuting, devaluing work, and devaluing faith—are signs of a compartmentalized life. We divide our existence into compartments with locked steel doors between them. What goes on in one room is completely separate from and irrelevant to what happens in the others. During the scandal of 1998, journalists stood in awe of President Clinton's legendary ability to compartmentalize his life. He could run the country, give leadership to Congress, and engage in international issues, while his private life became a mangled wreck. His ability to keep these worlds separate was considered evidence of his talent. Though keeping life's elements separate has been an effective coping mechanism for many—perhaps out of immediate necessity—compartmentalizing one's life long-term carries many difficulties and dangers for the Christian.

First of all, it is terribly inconsistent. Jesus called it hypocrisy (e.g., Matt. 23:25–28): saying you believe something and then turning around and violating that belief with expedient or self-serving action. This is moral schizophrenia, and the dissonance it causes in a person's heart and mind must eventually be resolved for a person to be healthy and whole! We cannot live an entire lifetime in this condition without serious instability.

Second, compartmentalizing is exhausting. The emotional drain of living a double life cannot be measured. It is hard enough to establish for myself a pattern of living without having to do it *twice*—once in private and once for the public eye! Personally, when I get really exhausted, my spiritual strength dissipates, and I am more likely to make mistakes and fall into sin.

Thirdly, compartmentalizing is unproductive. When I am unable to commit myself to a governing worldview based on truth and recognize an overarching purpose, my life becomes existentially meaningless. Solomon himself said, "All I have been striving for is an exercise in futility" (Eccl. 2:17, paraphrase). The question, Who am I, really? cannot be answered with confidence. A life without meaning comes to a profitless dead end.

So what is the Christian to do? If commuting and devaluing are not right or helpful, then what option is left? We can choose to bring all the aspects of our life under one umbrella. Some do this by adopting one organizing and empowering principle that will bring consistency, energy, and purpose to us. For countless millions around the world, this umbrella has been an ideology such as Marxism or capitalism; for others, the self reigns supreme.

The church, however, has given witness to Jesus Christ as the one who holds the key to life, and this he offers by giving himself to us as Savior and Lord. As God come in the flesh, Jesus brought us more than a mere organizing principle. He presented himself to us as the Person in whom we can find life itself. Recognizing the obstacle to that life—original sin and our unholy actions—Jesus presented himself as the One to reintroduce us to God through his atoning death on the cross. His redemptive work was so complete and so encompassing that we echo the apostle Peter's question, "Lord, to whom shall we go? You have the words of eternal life" (John 6:68, NIV).

And so we are invited to receive Jesus as Lord, which means simply that we let him be supreme over our own will, over our ideologies, over our possessions, over every other cheap substitute for God's reassuring presence. As we do so, we are invited to live literally *in him*, so to identify with him that we adopt his life as our own, his cross as our own, his resurrection as our own. We can do this because he has given himself to us. It seems to me now, in retrospect, that Solomon's downfall was losing his early trust of God and relying solely on his own success. We can avoid that fatal mistake by receiving Christ and living in him— which is the only viable option for the Christian. Christ transforms a compartmentalized life into a consecrated life, one that is turned over completely to his sovereign care. It is the only viable option, but it is a costly one, because it involves relinquishing to Jesus sovereignty over our destiny.

Let me illustrate. For Christmas a friend gave us a beautiful wrought-iron cross that stands upright. I wanted to think carefully about where this exquisite Christian symbol should be placed in our home, so I set it on our kitchen table and left it there until I could decide its permanent place.

Something very interesting started happening. This cross was always in the way.

My husband Andy usually gets up first in the morning and likes to spread the daily newspaper on the kitchen table to read while he eats breakfast. So the cross was moved to the edge of the table where it wouldn't disturb the paper. Then Katy and Judy, who come to the table later for breakfast, invariably moved the cross to another part of the table to make room for their meal. This shuffle continued the rest of the day. As the homework was spread out on the table, the cross was placed as far away as possible to give a clear work space. One of our family members even asked, "Can't we put this thing somewhere where it won't always be in the way?"

That's when I realized this humble cross was taking on new meaning in my life. Its presence was uncomfortable, because it represented my own sin and spiritual need. It became a constant reminder to me that God paid the price I deserved to pay, in order that I might be saved from the consequences of my sin. It revealed my desire to push spiritual things to the edge of my life rather than keeping Christ at the center. And it definitely got in the way of my defiant assumption that I can do things myself.

And so the wrought-iron cross found its permanent home—there in the middle of our kitchen table. We move it around, touch it, and allow it to remind us of our spiritual roots and God's strength. We've placed it where it can have its greatest power: at the center of our daily life, visible at all times, a reminder of the life we have been given in Jesus Christ, truly our Lord.

So let's say we are walking in Solomon's shoes, struggling with a life that is disjointed and inconsistent. What does the gospel hold out to us?

This life we have been given in Christ, of which Paul spoke to the church at Colossae, is a whole life, a consecrated life, a complete life. Nothing but sin is missing from it. With our roots set down deeply in Christ's life, we have just one life to live: a life wholly dedicated to him, fruitful and productive. Nothing is out of his reach or care. There is no inconsistency of values, no blurring of focus, just the peaceful sense his order brings to decisions, thoughts, and actions at home and in the world. In contrast to the moral schizophrenia of a compartmentalized life, life in Christ is morally strong and consistent. Jesus is the most stable influence we will ever know! The exhaustion of the compartmentalized life is replaced, in Christ, by the rejuvenating power of the Holy Spirit. We never again have to rely on our own strength for doing the right thing, because Jesus has provided an unlimited supply of power. The well of living water is never empty! In contrast to the meaninglessness of the compartmentalized life, eternal life in Christ has a purpose, a direction. We are pointed in joyful hope to the One who gave us everything and calls us to a response of grateful obedience!

This consecrated life is also a new life, in which we can expect nothing short of complete transformation! "If anyone is in Christ, he is a new creation; the old has gone, the new has come! All this is from God, who reconciled us to himself through Christ" (2 Cor. 5:17–18, NIV). Newness of life in Christ probably means some changes, a frightening prospect for some. But if we realize we're trading in confusion for clarity, exhaustion for energy, and futility for a glorious future, perhaps those transforming changes are worth going after.

New life means that we can actually know the mind of Christ—the wisdom of God—because God's "divine power has given us everything we need for life and godliness through our knowledge of him who called us by his own glory and goodness" (2 Peter 1:3, NIV). What an assurance for today's confused and inconsistent world!

New life in Christ means resurrection power is at work in our spirits. The apostle Paul, excited about this prospect, said, "If the Spirit of him who raised Jesus from the dead is living in you, he who raised Christ from the dead will also give life to your mortal bodies through his Spirit, who lives in you" (Rom. 8:11, NIV). Why waste incredible amounts of emotional energy trying to live a double life—one foot in the world, one foot in the kingdom of God—when what has been given to us is an inexhaustible supply of life-giving power, the kind that can revive the most tired, worn-out Christian for *effective* influence in the world!

New life in Christ enables us to live a holy life, one set apart and dedicated to the service of the One who created us, who loved us even when we were rebellious sinners, and who provided the means for our salvation. We cry out to Jesus, "Lord, Lord!" and by the enabling power of his Holy Spirit, we do what he says (Luke 6:46). This is our calling. This connects the dots of our life into one complete picture. This enables us to address the issues of everyday life, the problems at work, the stresses of family relationships, the inner struggles with sin, with the wisdom that comes from one sufficient source, Almighty God. Seeing every aspect of our existence under the Lordship of Christ allows us the simplicity of living just one life. What a gift has been given! Are you ready to receive it? May we each take hold of this precious blessing with gratitude and obedience! Amen.

NOTE

1. Doug Sherman and William Hendricks, *Your Work Matters to God* (Colorado Springs, Colo.: NavPress, 1987), 20–21.

PART 5

The Church,
the Body of Christ

The Unity We Seek
in the Midst of Our Diversity

An Evangelical Perspective

Jack Haberer

How odd to raise the subject. An evangelical perspective on unity in diversity? Evangelicals don't talk about it. They avoid the subject. After getting out the votes and scoring victories in battles over denominational standards on theology and ethics, and given the passion for the truths proclaimed in scripture, very few evangelicals in the Presbyterian Church (U.S.A.) are even willing to engage the subject of the nature of the unity that we seek in the midst of our diversity.

Never was the disinterest more obvious than when the 1998 General Assembly commissioned a conference by that name. Although Moderator Douglas Oldenberg recruited a half-dozen evangelicals to serve on the planning committee, only a few dozen additional evangelicals ultimately attended the conference. They were outnumbered by about twenty to one.

Why is there such disinterest? Evangelicals harbor the suspicion that unity in diversity is being promoted largely by liberal leaders who are trying to salvage their falling regime. It seems to be a convenient excuse to disregard the will of the more conservative majority.

Babel? . . . or Pentecost?

Then again, any evangelical will acknowledge that *cultural diversity* is a great thing. It results when the gospel is proclaimed beyond clannish borders. After the first Christian Pentecost, the Spirit drove that fledgling church to embrace "whosoever will come." Just as Jesus had bulldozed social barriers to scoop up lepers, prostitutes, and drunks, the apostolic church migrated from Jew to Gentile, from God-fearer to barbarian—all to the end of bringing God's plan of redemption to a lost world. Today, the presence in the church of many races offers demonstrable proof that the gospel is soaring on the winds of Pentecost.

It is *theological diversity* that makes evangelicals cringe. It results when well-intentioned, open-minded Christians embrace religious ideas and practices that depart from biblical teachings. Promoted by some in the academic community who have become enamored with the notion that all truth claims are equally valid (except those that claim to be superior to all others), all notions of divinity are accepted as equally valid, all names for gods are interchangeable. Even the content of such beliefs is prejudged to be equally valid, whether such propositions promote general well-being or ethnic cleansing. As one denominational official once said, "There are no good ideas or bad ideas, there are just your ideas and my ideas." The resulting relativism effectively promotes tribal deities much like those of ancient paganism. The first commandment, "thou shalt have no other gods before me," burns as hot against this idolatry today as it did against the golden calf in Moses' day.

Evangelicals draw a line between cultural diversity and an understanding of theological diversity that undercuts the gospel. It is, as it were, the difference between Pentecost and Babel. When God brings diverse people into the one fellowship of Christ and his church, Pentecost is re-engaged. But when humans, no matter how well-intentioned, disregard God's truth in order to form a religious fellowship of their own design, a tower of Babel results. The very unity sought becomes a disintegration realized.

To Tell the Truth

The major reason evangelicals disregard the subject of diversity is that they would much rather talk about the truth. Theologian Alister McGrath states that "the fundamental evangelical conviction has been that it is imperative to remain faithful to the gospel of Jesus Christ, and to allow no ideas or values from outside Christianity to exercise a normative role within its thought and life."[1] After surviving and even emerging victorious over the science-driven skepticism of the modernist movement, evangelicals are not about to succumb to the relativism of the postmodernist movement. As McGrath outlines it, evangelicals are committed to the truth because they trust scripture to be God's Word. While others may feel free to challenge all truth claims in scripture (and elsewhere), evangelicals consider that to do so is the height of arrogance. God's Word is truth, whether we like it, whether we understand it, or whether we obey it. All else is measured against the single standard of the gospel of Jesus Christ revealed through scripture.

The Problem with Denying Diversity

Then again, evangelicals do tolerate diversity of thought. Most have followed the maxim of the English Puritan pastor Richard Baxter (1615–91), "*In necessariis unitas, in non-necessariis libertas, in utrisque caritas*" (in essentials, unity; in non-essentials, freedom; and in all things, charity). This leads directly to the essential problem of the twentieth century. Just what are the essentials? What are the core values, the central beliefs, or, as termed a century ago, the fundamentals of Presbyterianism?

The fundamentalists of the 1920s did not provide a good answer. Though they tried valiantly to defend the orthodox faith, some of their efforts were misguided. As the theologian John Leith points out, "The fundamentalist-modernist controversies of the first half of this century fixed for the most part on many secondary doctrines. . . . The church's existence has never been dependent on a particular doctrine of verbal inerrancy, nor has it been dependent on the affirmation of the virgin birth as a historical fact."[2] Indeed, the fundamentalists killed the fundamentalist movement in the Presbyterian Church. When Gresham Machen sounded retreat in 1936 by leading a small band of allies out of the Presbyterian Church (U.S.A.), he thereby bequeathed the denomination's leadership to a broad coalition of liberals and moderates. Though many other conservatives remained, they found themselves relegated to ecclesiastical exile.

Gradually the neo-evangelical movement grew within the denomination, but these new evangelicals seemed willing to support an uneasy détente amid a wide diversity of beliefs in the church. When policies regarding remarriage of divorced persons were liberalized, disagreeing conservatives kept the fellowship intact. When the denomination opted to ordain women, some conservatives left, but most remained. In fact, many welcomed the change. Détente prevailed through debates on abortion, on ecumenical relationships, and on numerous politically partisan issues. More significantly, a respectful unity in diversity even bridged the chasm dividing the more liberal, neo-orthodox theology ("Scripture *reveals* the word of God") and the more conservative, neo-evangelical theology ("Scripture *is* the word of God").

How have evangelicals put up with such a tense peace? They have persisted, in part, by realizing that the antidote is worse than the poison. Clayton Bell, a leading champion of evangelicalism for forty years, reflects, "The damage caused by division is too devastating." After an eighteen-month battle to keep his 8,300-member Highland Park Presbyterian Church (Dallas, Texas) in the denomination, a sufficient block of votes was amassed in 1991 to decide to stay. However, a sizable minority left to form a congregation in the very conservative Presbyterian Church in America. "As folks on both sides tried to accumulate votes, deception overwhelmed honesty, false accusations flew, and mistreatment of one another nearly broke us," elaborates Bell. As if that were not costly enough, he adds that "families were divided over the vote. Years later, some relatives still are not on speaking terms. Worst yet," Bell continues, "at least one thousand members simply dropped out of church altogether. As best we can tell, most of them have not returned to any church. Many have given up on God." In sum, then: Given the choice between the horrors of schism and the tension of détente, let the tension continue.

On a more theological plane, the other reason many evangelicals eschew the horrors of schism and abide theological détente on so many topics is that doing so is consistent with the Bible's own teaching on the church. Scripture pronounces unqualified condemnation upon those who divide the church, especially when the divide is created by those claiming to be more spiritually and religiously pure. Paul wrote 1 Corinthians to a church where the "superspiritual" scorned those they considered "carnal" (the practice of incest among them suggests some accuracy in that assessment!). Should not the spiritually faithful pull away from such derelicts? Not so, says Paul: "Now I appeal to you, brothers and sisters, by the name of our Lord Jesus Christ, that all of you be in agreement and that there be no divisions among you, but that you be united in the same mind and the same purpose" (1 Cor. 1:10, NRSV). Paul understood Jesus' vision of the imperfect, sin-stained church. Jesus' parable said it simply: let the tares grow among the wheat for now, and ultimately God will separate them out (Matt. 13:24–30, 36–43). Of course, the church appropriately exercises discipline to restore those caught in a web of deception and rebellion, but to divide the church over such waywardness, or to try to purify the church by purging it of its most sinful sinners, is contrary to the teaching of scripture.

Churching It: as Anabaptists or as Reformed?

The desire to purify the church reminds one of a debate that raged during the Reformation. Martin Luther and John Calvin were committed to developing a church that was more faithful to the Word of God. Their progress was obvious. However, Calvin soon was challenged by the Anabaptists, who insisted that his church still was too brackish, too much a mix of sinners with saints. The Anabaptists' insistence upon believers' baptism grew not only from a literal reading of the Greek word, *baptizein* ("to immerse"). It also arose from their determination to allow into the church only those whose faith commitment and eternal salvation the leaders could confidently attest as genuine. Theirs was to be always and only the "community of the saved," as over against the "community of salvation" that Calvin was leading.

Calvin held no such perfectionist standards. All he claimed was that the church ought to be marked by faithful proclamation of the Word of God and right administration of the sacraments. In fact, "he readily acknowledges that even the marks themselves may be flawed. Some faults may well creep into either doctrine or sacraments, but this ought not estrange us from the communion of the church. . . . [Indeed] 'since all men are somewhat beclouded with ignorance, either we must leave no church remaining or we must condone delusion in those matters which can go unknown without harm to the sum of religion and without loss of salvation.' "[3]

Calvin's acceptance of such flaws explains the difference he drew between the "visible church" and the "invisible church." He assumed that the organizational church would include both wheat and tares, while trusting that God alone knew who was elect for eternal blessing. Bringing all that debate into the present, one can see that attempts to divide the church between the true believers and the untrue, between the biblical and the apostate, between the moral and the amoral, reflect an Anabaptist ecclesiology, not a Reformed one. As is sometimes evidenced by the other small denominations that have severed ties with the PC(USA), self-righteousness and pharisaism follow like the tail behind the dog.

Whence Cometh This Diversity?

The most common way to summarize our divisions is by borrowing the political categories of liberals vs. conservatives. The fundamentalist-modernist controversy launched such two-party thinking. On the conservative side, Gresham Machen drew the line clearly and called for a division of the house: "A separation between the two parties in the Church is the crying need of the hour."[4] The lines were drawn just as clearly on the liberal side by C. C. Morrison, the editor of *The Christian Century*. In an editorial titled "Fundamentalism and Modernism: Two Religions" he stated, "The God of the fundamentalist is one God; the God of the modernist is another. . . ." He concluded, "The inherent incompatibility of the two worlds has passed the stage of mutual tolerance."[5] There is one problem with such categorizations, however. Most Presbyterians shun labels like "fundamentalist" or "liberal." Many Presbyterians choose their convictions on a case-by-case basis, not by party platform.

The sociologist William Weston has suggested that the Presbyterian Church is comprised of three parties. Roughly 10 percent are liberals intent on modifying the church's beliefs. A second ten percent are conservatives intent on protecting beliefs. And eighty percent are moderates who cast the deciding votes on the issues raised by the liberals and conservatives.[6] Given that most Presbyterians happily claim to be moderates, the 80 percent figure may be understated. However, that large middle group has wide differences within it and defies realistic identification as a single party. While this three-party paradigm helps push beyond the even more simplistic two-party model, it still trivializes the agendas of both liberals and conservatives while too easily amassing a middle that is itself sharply divided.

The diversity of beliefs held with such intensity by sincere faith-opponents begs for a better conceptualization. We need to find a better way to explain the diverse ways scripture is quoted by people talking past one another, as if they were speaking two different languages. We need to understand why so many Presbyterians bristle on some issues yet do not want to be categorized as allies with many others who bristle in the same way. Perhaps our differences lie in the way believers are driven by their *theo-ideological impulses.*

Five Theo-ideological Impulses

What is a theo-ideological impulse? First of all, an impulse is an immediate, internal inclination to act in a particular way, rooted in part in temperament and in part in environment. It is shaped by education and experience, intensified and amended both by positive reinforcement and negative consequences. For believers, those impulses are especially influenced by joining an ideologically driven group, like Presbyterians Pro-Life or Voices of Sophia. As advocacy groups sharpen and intensify a person's values, those values form the measuring standards by which other ideas are evaluated. To use a philosophical term, they become the a priori assumptions, the essential beliefs upon which all other beliefs are built. They are so deeply dyed into the lens of one's eyes that they color everything one sees. These impulses are so essential to one's internal belief structure that they are almost beyond criticism, and even may be beyond perception.

Theo-ideological impulses are held even more intensely because they have been shaped by one's belief in God. Indeed, these impulses largely grow out of one's sense of "what God is up to," that is, what God is aiming to accomplish in the world.

Curiously, within the Christian community, believers give evidence of different sets of beliefs, different theo-ideological impulses. Categorically speaking, there seem to have emerged in our day five distinct impulses. Many believers can probably see some merit in all five, but they also see major flaws in positions promoted by those following impulses they resist. Some will find two or more impulses surging within them. Most believers, however, are driven especially by just one of these impulses:

> *The inclusivist impulse*: the conviction that God is about the business of welcoming. The central task of faith is to break down walls between people, open doors to outsiders, and, in the process, unmask the power of privileged insiders.
> *The beneficent impulse*: the conviction that God is about the business of compassion and charity. The central task of faith is to extend mercy to the hungry, the sick, the poor, and the abandoned, and to provide the community a moral conscience.
> *The loyalist impulse*: the conviction that God is about the business of strengthening the faith community. The central task of faith is to build up the church, to loyally sup-

port its ministries, to bring peace among its warring factions, and to exercise sound judgment in its community life.

The renewalist impulse: the conviction that God is about the business of bringing people into a personal relationship with the Lord. The central task of faith is to share the gospel with unbelievers and to foster an ever-deepening, spiritually vital relationship with God through prayer, worship, and personal Bible study.

The confessional impulse: the conviction that God is about the business of advancing the truth. The central task of faith is to study and rightly teach the Word of God, to guard the orthodox faith against erroneous teachings, and, in the process, to unmask the purveyors of error in doctrine and immorality in ethics.

A person driven by one impulse may likely misunderstand those driven by other impulses. Nevertheless, each impulse is rooted deeply within Christian tradition and is found in scripture itself. Each has grown deeply within Christians' souls because each impulse is taught by the Word of God.

Many evangelicals tend toward the confessional impulse. "You will know the truth, and the truth will set you free" (John 8:32, NIV). That truth, revealed in Jesus Christ and attested in scripture, is evidence enough that one must hold to the proclamation of the Word on God's terms. No wonder the Bible condemns those who turn from the truth to follow other gods and other teachings!

Then again, many evangelicals tend toward the softer, gentler renewalist impulse. "Go and make disciples of all nations" (Matt. 28:19, NIV). While supporting the confessional effort, the renewalist is not likely to take up arms to oppose heresy. Rather, she or he can be found in a prayer meeting or a group Bible study or seminar on how to share the faith. To know God and to make God known, to fully fulfill Jesus' central command to "love the Lord with all your heart and with all your soul and with all your mind" (Matt. 22:37, NIV): thus yearns the renewalist.

Fewer evangelicals are prodded by the loyalist impulse. Mere passive, institutional Christianity holds little attraction for the evangelical. However, this impulse draws from the deep well of biblical teaching regarding unity within the church. Underlined by Jesus' prayer "that they may be one" (John 17:11, NIV), the apostles urge strenuous efforts to keep the church together, indeed, to keep the whole Christian movement together.

Arising from the more liberal side of the church is the beneficent impulse. Again, some evangelicals remain critical of social activism. Jesus, however, teaches that "whatever you did for one of the least of these . . . you did for me" (Matt. 25:40, NIV). Touched by the enormous compassion demonstrated by Jesus, inspired by Jesus' healing of the sick, and pressed by the prophets (Seek justice, love mercy, and walk humbly with your God, Micah 6:8), the beneficent impulse constantly presses to put love into action.

The most liberal impulse is the inclusivist. Here evangelicals commonly run headlong into the relativistic, multicultural pluralism that questions if Jesus really is the only way to God. However, this impulse, too, is rooted deeply in scripture—from God's plan for Abraham and Sarah to be a blessing to all nations, to the extraordinarily inclusive, multilingual congregation born on Pentecost; from Peter's vision overturning the kosher dietary laws with the words, "what God has made clean, you must not call profane" (Acts 10:15), to Paul's proclamation that "there is neither Jew nor Greek, there is neither slave nor free, neither male nor female, for you are all one in Christ Jesus" (Gal. 3:28, NIV).

Corralling These Impulses

The question naturally arises whether all these impulses may simply be followed as they arise. Each impulse probably has been born in the hearts of believers by the formative powers of Christian upbringing and by the influences of a culture still echoing some of the religious proclamations on which it was built. But each impulse also can lead persons into error.

As stated earlier, inclusivity toward persons is appropriate. Let all persons find an open door welcoming them into Christ's church. Yet inclusivity toward ideas foreign to the gospel is usually precarious and often heretical. The inclusivist impulse has theological limits.

The beneficent impulse is dangerous in a more subtle way. While it tends to the physical needs of the poor, it often neglects the person's soul. By treating so many issues on socioeconomic terms only, charitable ministries often fail to address the issues of personal salvation. The recipients of the charity frequently return to their prior state unless their hearts are changed by a relationship with God.

The loyalist impulse can be thanked for holding the church together through conflicts, but it tends to put structures before substance, trust before truth, and peace before purity. The person holding to the loyalist impulse will assert the virtue of the polity of the Presbyterian Church while paying little attention to the gospel the church needs to proclaim. The loyalist impulse can drive the church into irrelevance.

Renewal fell into disrepute through much of the twentieth century, due to its disregard of the social crises of the day. Just as James chides the offering of prayer alone to the hungry (they need food, too!—2:14–17), the renewalist impulse can lead to wondrous spiritual experiences that are divorced from real life.

The confessional impulse certainly can protect the accuracy of doctrines. But how much accuracy is even possible? Calvin said that there has never been a theology that is more than 70 percent correct. If Christian theology were so self-evident, why then are so many theologies being written, even within the evangelical community? Further, confidence in the truth often leads to feelings of contempt toward all those who do not hold to the same truth in the same way. Judgmentalism and triumphalism—the dismissal of all alternate opinions as falsehoods—tend to be pervasive among those with a confessional impulse. They have alienated even many of their renewalist allies. "The insolence of Christians who exalt their own understanding of Christian faith while barely acknowledging the faithfulness of those with different understandings is a scandal that holds Christianity up to the contempt of the world."[7]

The question arises whether any of these impulses can be trusted. In one sense, all of them—and none of them—can be trusted. You need to listen within yourself to discern which impulse(s) are most in evidence. At the same time you need to listen to the others—other believers, other churches, other organizations, other enclaves of agreement—to discern more clearly your own and others' impulses. You must listen respectfully to perceive the best intentions in yourself and others. You must listen discerningly to perceive the errors of judgment and the errors of intention that the chaff within us and among us has sown and grown. On occasion, you must note when a person's faith has so totally stepped outside the parameters of orthodoxy as to be truly heretical. Likewise, when someone's behavior has wandered outside the range of Christian ethics, morals, or manners, the situation may require speaking the truth in love to seek restoration to the flock.

When surveying the diversity in the church on these terms, we can see why in so many debates the speakers talk past each other. It is no wonder that a person with an inclusivist impulse cannot comprehend the passions of the confessional-impulsed person—and vice versa. They are traveling on different tracks. If, however, they are willing to talk together and listen together, allowing their diversity to mutually inform their theo-ideologies and even amend their theo-ideological impulses, maybe the church can find a way to live more truly in unity amid diversity.

A Few Suggestions

First, recognize the essential validity and potential value found in each of the five theo-ideological impulses. The church needs people who constantly push open our doors to the excluded just as much as it needs those who will fight to preserve the truth. It needs those who zealously care for the needy just as much as it needs those who are passionate in their love for God. And in the midst of the rest, it needs those other persons who constantly study the peace of the fellowship.

By affirming the good intentions of those with whom we disagree, and by acknowledging some of the negative tendencies that crop up from all our ideologies, we open the door to serious engagement and genuine learning by all of us. When we are so secure in our convictions that we need no longer to hold defensively to them, we are better able to allow God to shape them into beliefs and ideologies more consistent with the full counsel of God in scripture. None of us, save God alone, understands the whole truth completely. We need to break out of our impoverished enclaves of agreement in order to allow the larger Christian community to help hone our understanding. What great learning happens when we all engage in a mutual prophecy of speaking the truth in love (as each of us sees it), all the while seeking to discern the voice of God. The church can avoid balkanization only when people representing competing viewpoints engage in dialogue together rather than fighting against each other.

Second, re-engage the text of scripture. All theo-ideologies are guilty of quoting scripture out of context or in truncated fashion. Indeed, all biblical students are selective literalists, because each impulse and each resulting mindset has grown out of one theme of biblical teaching, but often to the neglect of other themes. Ultimately, every idea must be taken captive to Christ. Every truth claim, every theological and moral proposition, must be informed and measured by the whole counsel of God, with scripture interpreting scripture.

Third, promote a unity that is historical as well as geographical. While some advocate unity amid diverse contemporary beliefs we ought to advocate unity with historic beliefs too. The "Union in Christ" declaration begins with the words, "With the witness of Scripture and the Church through the ages we declare . . ." This point is enlarged in the third article: "We turn away from forms of Church life that discount the authority of Scripture or claim knowledge of God that is contrary to the full testimony of Scripture as interpreted by the Holy Spirit working in and through the community of faith across time." The fifth article adds: "By our union in Christ the Church binds together believers in every time and place. . . . We also turn away from

forms of Church life that ignore the witness of those who have
gone before us." Evangelicals' concern to maintain truth, at least
in part, grows out of a concern to hold to the teachings of the
church through the ages. It stands as an appropriate counter to
"modern chauvinism," the haughty arrogance pervading the
scholarly world that "assumes the intrinsic inferiority of all pre-
modern wisdoms."[8]

*Fourth, reclaim the center of the church's theological discus-
sion.* After losing the fundamentalist-modernist controversy,
evangelicals have struggled to recover the center of the theological discussion. One way to begin is to acknowledge that the fundamentalists were wrong. We need not repeat their failed
attempt to protect secondary doctrines under assault in a particular way at a particular time. Rather, the task of "the preserva-
tion of the truth" demands that we articulate faithfully the truly
suprahistorical truths that stand at the center of the faith. Such
truths have been outlined in the Nicene Creed and the church's
teaching on the doctrine of the Trinity. Such truths are found in
the core teachings of the Reformers, summed up under the
rubrics *sola scriptura, sola gratia,* and *solus Christus.* Such
truths have been developed in such efforts as "Union in Christ:
A Declaration for the Church." Such truths can and must lead to
genuine theological studies. Evangelicals ought to shout such
truths from the housetops.

Evangelicals have good reason to proclaim the gospel confidently. After years of exile to the outer reaches of Presbyterian
church life, they need to take notice of the remarkable structural
changes that have been taking place. The bankruptcy of many
revisionist programs has negated the core of influence once held
by the inclusivist-beneficent-loyalist hegemony in mainline
Presbyterianism. The strength of Christ-centered proclamation
has magnetically drawn evangelicals to the center of denominational leadership, and it promises only to strengthen that leadership. Evangelicals can speak more authoritatively, more convinc-
ingly, and more graciously—even within the halls of liberal
establishments—because they have the attention of the formerly
powerful monopoly. Simply put, while fueled by their proclama-

tion of Jesus Christ at the center, evangelicals need to live in the center, acting like the church rather than an opposition party.

Fifth, by all means proclaim Christ! The center of the faith is Jesus Christ, both the historical facts of the life of Jesus the Christ and the redemptive power of Christ the Lord. As the instructive General Assembly policy paper *Is Christ Divided?* says,

> Unity depends upon common loyalty. For Christians the object of that loyalty is not a proposition or an institution, but the person of Jesus Christ. . . . Any expression of faith which fails to affirm faith in Jesus Christ has crossed the boundary and is no longer Christian faith. To say this is to do more than mouth a formality, for the declaration "Jesus Christ" is a confession of faith in an identifiable reality. As we have already seen, a central affirmation of the New Testament's witness is that the Jesus of history and the risen Christ are one: The teller of parables is the exalted Lord; the Living Christ is the one who ate and drank with sinners. This essential continuity between Jesus of Nazareth and Christ the Lord must not be broken.[9]

Evangelicals, served by the theologically minded confessional impulse and the spiritually minded renewalist impulse, have been passionate about declaring Jesus Christ as revealed in scripture. As always, the need is great for this center of the faith to be proclaimed loudly. Evangelicals' insistence on maintaining a Christocentric faith that affirms the absolute uniqueness of Christ's revelation and redemption must never be muted.

Sixth, mind your manners. My mother taught me to treat people the way I would like to be treated. She taught me to listen before speaking. She taught me to check the facts before drawing conclusions. She taught me to try to trust others' intentions, no matter how ill-advised might be their actions. She taught me to express my words as graciously as possible, giving the maximum amount of information while minimizing the amount of threat to the other person. I learned those lessons well as a child, but as an adult I have sometimes felt I was exempt from following them. I am not. None of us is. Jesus taught almost all of those lessons, as did the apostles.

If we evangelicals are going to claim to be "more biblical," that claim must be just as true of our manners as it is of our orthodoxy. Otherwise we are frauds. The church will never purify its theology by using slander as its methodology. Rather, when we believe someone is teaching flawed theology, we ought to obey Jesus' instruction: to confront the person first in private in the hope of winning that person back to the truth. If we are unsuccessful on the first attempt, we are to confront the person again with two or three others as witnesses. Finally, if our efforts continue unsuccessfully, we are to confront the person publicly (Matt. 18:15–17). Jesus did not say, "When you catch someone in a fault, write about it in a searing editorial and publish as widely as possible." We need to mind our manners; we need to obey the teachings of scripture.

The Imperative

Many evangelicals really could be quite happy never to have to discuss the issue of unity and diversity. It is easier just to preach the gospel, to huddle within our own enclave of agreement, and to rehearse a comfortable faith with one another. But if we distance ourselves from those with whom we differ in Christ, we become impoverished spiritually and theologically. We need to learn from the insights and challenges of those with whom we disagree, and they need the benefit of our learning. Together we learn and grow. Together we can participate in a church that collectively hears the voice of God, mediates wisdom where it would otherwise produce foolishness, and passes to the next generation a healthier, better-informed faith. We evangelicals may prefer to avoid the subject, but facing it is the imperative of the gospel.

NOTES

1. Alister McGrath, *A Passion for Truth: The Intellectual Coherence of Evangelicalism* (Downers Grove, Ill.: InterVarsity Press, 1996), 241.

2. John Leith, *Crisis in the Church: The Plight of Theological Education* (Louisville, Ky.: Westminster John Knox Press, 1997), 29.
3. *Is Christ Divided?* (Louisville, Ky.: Presbyterian Church [U.S.A.], 1988), 7.
4. J. Gresham Machen, *Christianity and Liberalism* (New York: Macmillan Co., 1923), 160.
5. *The Christian Century* (Jan. 3, 1924), 6.
6. See William Weston, *Presbyterian Pluralism: Competition in a Protestant House* (Knoxville: Univ. of Tennessee Press, 1997).
7. *Is Christ Divided?* 41.
8. Thomas Oden, *Requiem: A Lament in Three Movements* (Nashville: Abingdon Press, 1995), 133.
9. *Is Christ Divided?* 7, 38.

The Mission of the Church

Sherron George

"God so loved the world . . ."

W hich comes first, church or mission? Does the church have a mission, or does mission have a church? For centuries the focus has been on *the church's mission*, and at times only on the church—her doctrine, purity, and internal use of Word and sacrament. Church was perceived as a "place where" certain things happen, and mission was reduced to an appendage or special interest of a passionate few volunteers. In recent times theologians Karl Barth, Jürgen Moltmann, David Bosch, and Lesslie Newbigin have taught that it would be more biblical to speak about *the mission's church*. Whose mission?

God's mission! The triune God has a gracious mission in relation to fallen humanity that begins in Genesis 3 with the call, "Where are you?" That mission will be consummated when every tongue confesses, "Jesus is Lord," and the integrity of creation is restored. God's universal mission of restoration, salvation, forgiveness, liberation, healing, and reconciliation unfolds in human history, forms a covenant people to be a witness to the nations, sends a Savior to redeem humankind, sends the Spirit upon all flesh with gifts of communion and empowerment, and establishes a church that is an instrument of God's mission to the world and for the world.

Missio Dei (the mission of God) originates in God's heart, God's person, God's activity, God's love. "For God so loved the world that God gave his only Son . . ." (John 3:16). *Missio Dei* is Trinitarian, a mission partnership of the three persons of the Trinity. It is highly significant that the "Union in Christ" declaration *begins* with these words: "Jesus Christ is the gracious mission of God to the world and for the world."

God's mission seeks and sends. As God sent Jesus and the Spirit, so God sends the church into the world as one agent of God's missionary purpose (John 17:18; 20:21). Therefore, "to participate in mission is to participate in the movement of God's love toward people, since God is a fountain of sending love."[1] The Latin word *missio* and the English *mission* translate two New Testament Greek verbs for "to send" (*apostellein* and *pempein*). Both Greek verbs are used in John 20:21, "As the father has sent (*apestalken*) me, so I send (*pempo*) you." In Jesus' great missionary prayer in John 17 the verb "to send" (*apostellein*) is used seven times, including twice in verse 18, "As you have sent me . . . so I have sent them."[2] The noun form in English is *apostle*. An apostle in the Bible is "one who is sent" with a mission.

As the incarnate body of Jesus Christ was sent into the world in the first century, so is the local-global ecclesial or missional body of Jesus Christ (the church) sent into the world today. As the first-century apostles were sent "to the ends of the earth," so the "one, holy, catholic, and *apostolic* Church" is sent in mission. *Apostolic* is not necessarily related to "apostolic succession," but to apostolic foundation, commission, and activity or "sentness."[3]

Why is it important to change traditional conceptions and insist that mission comes before church, that mission drives the church, rather than the church driving mission? Because only then does it become clear that, along with the praise of God, the primary reason and purpose of the church's existence is mission. The church's nature is *missional* or *apostolic*. God's mission has a church. It is radical to move from having a "church-centered" mission to being a "mission-centered" or missional church. The emphasis changes from "sending" to "being sent."

In his landmark work *Transforming Mission*, David Bosch aptly clarifies that the church is neither "the *ground* of mission" nor "the *goal* of mission," and must continually remember her "*provisional* character" as an object, instrument, witness, and sign of God's missionary love and reign.[4] The goal of God's mission is captured in the opening words of the Lord's Prayer: "Hallowed be your name; your kingdom come . . ." Mission is for the glory of God and the establishment of the reign of God on earth and in heaven. The ultimate aim of mission and evangelism is the glory of God. The church is not the end. Proselytism is not the end. Missionary activity and church growth are not the ends. By bearing faithful witness to Christ, the church glorifies God, who calls her to mission partnership.

The church is composed of those whom God "calls out" of the world and brings together for worship, nurture, preparation, and fellowship in order to be sent back into the world "to proclaim the mighty acts of him who called you out of darkness into his marvelous light" (1 Peter 2:9, NRSV). Bosch conceives of the church as "a body of people sent on a mission." This new way of understanding church and mission is thoroughly explicated in *Missional Church*, which states: "Unlike the previous notion of the church as an entity located in a facility or in an institutional organization and its activities, the church is being reconceived as a community, a gathered people, brought together by a common calling and vocation to be a *sent people*.[5]

Karl Barth portrays the Holy Spirit gathering, upbuilding, and sending the Christian community.[6] Loren Mead envisions an alternating rhythm of discipleship within the local congregation and apostolate in the world.[7] The *Book of Order*, under "The Church and Its Mission," demonstrates how the church is called out of and sent into the world (G-3.0300):

> The Church is called to tell the good news of salvation by the grace of God through faith in Jesus Christ as the only Savior and Lord, proclaiming in Word and Sacrament.
> The Church is called to present the claims of Jesus Christ,

leading persons to repentance, acceptance of him as Savior and Lord, and new life as his disciples.

The Church is called to be Christ's faithful evangelist going into the world, making disciples of all nations.

The church is both "catholic" (there is one universal, global church) and "particular" (there are many local congregations). The church that started in Jerusalem is now a truly global church organized into strong, autonomous denominations and local churches doing mission in six continents. The churches in each nation have primary responsibility for mission in that country. Denominations participate in God's mission at national and global levels and facilitate, advise, and guide the mission endeavors of particular congregations. This is stated well in *Missional Church*: "A now-global church recognize[s] that the church of any place bears missional calling and responsibility for its own place as well as for distant places. The church of every place . . . is a mission-sending church, and the place of every church is a mission-receiving place."[8]

Every local congregation is a primal agent in God's mission. Lesslie Newbigin affirms that the "hermeneutic of the gospel is a congregation of men and women who believe it and live by it."[9] Today localism or decentralized mission is a strong trend, as local congregations assume more missional responsibility and identity. Particular churches engage in local and global mission in partnership with their regional and denominational mission agencies, with other churches and religious groups in their local community, with government and nongovernmental agencies, with other mission organizations, with indigenous partner churches in other nations around the world, with the poor and marginalized, with people of other faiths, with missionaries from around the world, and with local and global ecumenical agencies. God's mission is always done in partnerships and with local-global implications.

What?

Part V of the "Union in Christ" declaration states, "By our union with Christ our lives participate in God's mission to the world." What does it mean for the church to "participate in

God's mission to the world"? What is mission? During the twentieth century, due to church decline, cultural shifts, theological
pluralism, and organizational changes, the consensus and clarity
that Presbyterians had in relation to the nature and importance
of mission and evangelism have been "eroded by a contentious
debate over mission priorities."[10] When denominations shifted to
corporate programmatic church models, mission and evangelism
became programs among many options and priorities, and the
understanding of mission became clouded and confused.
Stephen Neill warned, "When everything is mission, nothing is
mission."

After teaching mission in a PC(USA) seminary for three years
now and reflecting on my twenty-three years of experience as a
PC(USA) mission co-worker in Brazil, I have come to one
astounding conclusion. We lack a clear definition of mission. The
old definition of mission as the Western church imperialistically
sending missionaries to distant places is not viable any longer.
What is mission today?

G. Thompson Brown uses the Latin *missio* and says, "The
church 'in mission' is God's missile or projectile which is hurled
into the world. . . . 'Mission,' then, is the church in motion, the
activity of the church as it is sent into the world ."[11] John R. W.
Stott defines mission as "everything the church is sent into the
world to do."[12] "Being sent" definitely involves crossing a frontier
or boundary. There are many kinds of frontiers or barriers that
are crossed, but the basic one is the door of the church. The
"world" is the mission field that begins outside the front door of
the church. Mission is "being sent" as light, salt, servant, prophet,
and witness to those "outside" one's church fellowship, especially
to those who are different from those inside. My working definition begins like this: *Mission is everything the local-global
church is sent into the world to be and do as a participant in
God's mission.*

However, something is still missing. Mission is not only being
sent. It is also receiving. In the past, mission was one-way, hier-
archical, and monological in a way that fostered attitudes of
superiority, inferiority, control, and dependency. Anthony Gittins

in *Bread for the Journey* defines mission as an attitude that is dialogical, incarnational, respectful of the cultural identity of others, that gets beyond the binary mentality of "us" and "them."[13] He calls for "Mission in Reverse," which Claude-Marie Barbour describes this way:

> The mission-in-reverse approach teaches that the minister can and should learn from the people ministered to—including, and perhaps especially, from the poor and marginalized people. By taking these people seriously, by listening to them . . . personal relationships are developed, and the dignity of the people is enhanced. Such presence to people is seen as necessarily allowing them to be the leaders in the relationship."[14]

This kind of two-way mission requires humility, relationships, reciprocity, and responsiveness. Gittins and Bosch insist that mission is mutually transforming, giving and receiving, being sent and being transformed. Jesus instructs missioners to take no bread or money, in order first to receive a cup of cold water and hospitality. He demonstrates this reality as he receives from Martha and Mary, the Samaritan woman, and Zacchaeus. He also talks about receiving the kingdom of God as a child.

Therefore my complete definition is this: *Mission is everything the local-global church is sent into the world to be and do as a participant in God's mission and everyone the local-global church receives in Christ's name and way.*

"Everything" and "everyone" are broad terms that need to be specified. Orlando Costas insists that mission must be "holistic" or seen in its totality in order to maintain its integrity. Through holistic mission we share the whole gospel with the whole person in the whole world. If mission is the apostolic vocation of the church in the world in partnership with God and others, what activities comprise holistic mission? "Everything" encompasses a diverse gamut of local-global missional activities that always include three vital areas: evangelism, social justice, and compassionate service.[15]

Jesus exemplified God's holistic mission. The Synoptic

Gospels frequently speak of three activities in Jesus' work—proclaiming, teaching, and healing (Matt. 4:23; 9:35)—which also became the vocation of the disciples.[16] Jesus began his public ministry "proclaiming the good news (*euangelion*) of God, and saying, 'The time is fulfilled, and the kingdom of God has come near; repent, and believe in the good news' " (Mark 1:14–15, NRSV). *Evangelism* is the proclamation, communication, or sharing in word and deed of the good news of the love and saving grace of God. The church has a vocation to proclaim the gospel (*euangelion*) of Jesus Christ to all peoples. Evangelization includes a gracious invitation (without imposition or exaltation) and a call to decision and discipleship in the context of a faith community.

In addition to proclaiming the good news and teaching, Jesus engaged in mission by "curing every disease and every sickness. When he saw the crowds, he had compassion for them, because they were harassed and helpless, like sheep without a shepherd" (Matt. 9:35–36). He engaged in ministries of healing and compassionate *service*. The program areas of the Worldwide Ministries' Global Service and Witness demonstrate a range of such mission activities: education and leadership development, evangelism, health ministries, hunger, disaster assistance and refugee resettlement, and self-development of peoples. Mission entails all of these areas.

It is obvious that Jesus' mission also included social *justice* or liberation of those suffering from economic, political, or spiritual oppression. In his inaugural sermon in Nazareth, Jesus used the words of Isaiah to define his mission: "The Spirit of the Lord . . . has anointed me to bring good news to the poor. He has sent me to proclaim release to the captives and recovery of sight to the blind, to let the oppressed go free, to proclaim the year of the Lord's favor" (Luke 4:18–19, NRSV). Mission as social justice involves dealing with all forms of institutional racism and discrimination. It is a call to reconciliation and peacemaking and an engagement in social policy at all levels. Mission not only reduces welfare rolls but reforms welfare systems and enables the self-development and empowerment of the poor. Many

Presbyterian congregations in the United States do a notable local mission work as social service or assistance but have not yet engaged in the root causes and cures as political action for social justice.

The vocational calling of the local-global church is holistic mission that includes activities of evangelism, service, and justice.

When?

Jesus proclaimed, "The time is fulfilled, and the kingdom of God has come near," and taught his disciples to pray, "Your kingdom come." Thus he demonstrated that God's mission is eschatological. What does that mean? Jesus inaugurated a new reality, a new life, a new creation that is "already" here but "not yet" complete. God's reign of love, justice, peace, and integrity is present, though at times hidden. When Jesus completed his mission, he ascended to the right hand of God, the Spirit came down at Pentecost, and the church was born to continue God's mission "in between" the ascension and return of Christ. During this interim the church is called to practice now the values of the reign of God in order to be a *sign* of it for the world and to participate in God's mission. This requires an urgent patience or patient urgency. In a world of much bad news and despair, there is a message of good news and hope to share!

Where?

Jesus "finished" (John 17:4; 19:30) the mission that God sent him to accomplish "outside the gate" (Heb. 13:13) "where the leftovers of cultic sacrifice were thrown."[17] Orlando Costas says this proves that the suffering and risen Lord "is to be located in the battles and heat of history, among the nonpersons of society."[18] Costas evokes liberation for the oppressed Latin American continent and declares the United States as a mission field, a new Macedonia, for Third World Christians. "Since Jesus died outside the gate," Costas contends, "mission has become the crossing of the walls and gates of our secured and comfortable compounds . . . encountering the crucified Christ in the world of the outsiders and sharing in his suffering for the rejects and outcasts."[19] The mission field begins when Christians leave the sanctuary and encounter "outsiders" in God's world. Those on the margins of society receive special attention in God's mission.[20]

Another image for the mission field derives from the command to love "your neighbor as yourself" (Luke 10:28). A church engages in mission when it loves and cares for those outside its fellowship as it loves and cares for its own members. A congregation might inquire, as did the young lawyer, "And who is my neighbor?" (Luke 10:29) or "Where is my neighbor?" The neighbors to be loved are in the church's immediate neighborhood, city, county, neighboring states or countries, and around the world. How many people like poor Lazarus are there at our gates (Luke 16:19)? How many people like the crippled beggar do we pass "at the gate of the temple" (Acts 3:2)? Mission simply means loving and serving those outside one's local church as we love and serve our members, doing unto others as we do to our own.

The church is sent outside her doors to engage in mission locally, nationally, and globally. Where does she receive "everyone in Christ's name and way"? At the gates. The Hebrews were enjoined to welcome the stranger. New and different people are always coming to our country, state, city, neighborhood, and church. Receiving and welcoming these strangers with their unique gifts and cultures is mission. It includes hospitality evangelism, new member assimilation, and mission in reverse. Seekers become Christians, and newcomers find a church home. Church leaders from other cultures and countries are received as missionaries who bring a fresh cutting-edge perspective and have much to teach about spirituality, ethics, and mission. As congregations do local mission outside their front door, the global community, the poor, and the marginalized become partners in mutual mission, not objects of mission or strangers to be ignored. Churches embrace people from other countries in their communities as God's gifts and missionary agents to them. The results of church as a "mission-receiving place" are spiritual and numerical growth, multicultural worship, and a global perspective that facilitates prayer, dialogue, relationships, and mission.

Who?

Mission is not something done "to" or "for" others, but "with" others. We participate in God's mission in loving communion with: (1) the triune God who empowers, sends, and directs us; (2) one another in the local-global church; and (3) those to whom we are sent and those whom we receive. Bosch speaks of mission as "the church-with-others,"[21] the church in solidarity with the world. In order to further clarify the nature of the mission enterprise, those to whom the local-global church is sent and whom she receives can be divided into four categories: (1) the unreached; (2) the unchurched; (3) other churches; and (4) people of other faiths. With each of these groups the emphasis on mission as evangelism, justice, and service may vary.

The *unreached* are non-Christians who have either never heard the gospel of Jesus Christ, never understood it, or never made a decision to accept Christ as Savior and Lord. While all justice and service mission projects indiscriminately include the unreached, an essential activity that cannot be neglected is evangelism. This group can further be divided into those who have and those who do not have access to the gospel and a witnessing church. There are many ways of evangelizing friends, neighbors, colleagues, strangers, and acquaintances—by word and deed, personal faith sharing, literature, invitations, and daily witness. Congregations utilize seeker services, media, visitation, and hospitality. Cross-cultural mission workers are sent to groups who have no Christian church nearby. Where public or explicit evangelism is not allowed, mission workers engage in service activities in the areas of education, health, and community development.

The *unchurched* include a constituency whom Walter Brueggemann describes as "*insiders* to the faith who have grown careless, weary, jaded, and cynical about the faith,"[22] but who also need evangelizing. In the United States, Canada, and Europe, a major thrust of evangelism and service is with the unchurched or nominal Christians. While one important way to evangelize the unchurched is by warmly welcoming and authentically receiving them when they come as visitors, church members must proactively invite them to church and intentionally seek to engage them in significant gospel conversations in daily life settings. Some congregations have designed special services directed to the needs and language of the unchurched. All churches must be aware of communication and cultural issues that can keep the unreached and unchurched from understanding the gospel and participating in the worship service. Most mission service projects seek to meet the immediate physical, material, and economic needs of poor and marginal people, many of whom are unchurched. It is important to treat them with dignity, respect, and compassion, and to remember that holistic mission also includes evangelism and justice.

Mission with *other churches* mainly involves service or justice activities. Service projects include short-term mission trips with congregations in neighbor communities, states, or countries that collaborate in responding to disasters or in constructing needed facilities. The validity of these projects is contingent on the quality of relationships and interaction with the neighbor churches. Health professionals, educators, and community developers are often invited by partner churches around the world to join their professionals in hospitals, schools, seminaries, and ecumenical agencies. In the quest for social justice as reconciliation between races and ethnicities, intentional dialogue and joint worship, fellowship, and mission experiences are productive. Churches unite their mission efforts denominationally and ecumenically around causes and programs that combat AIDS, violence, hunger, hate crimes, racism, poverty, and all forms of oppression. Support and nesting of new immigrant fellowships are evangelistic partnerships in mission.

Mission with *people of other faiths* entails three distinct activities: service and justice projects together, dialogue, and witness. People of all faiths and ideologies can join forces in seeking justice, peace, and reconciliation in their communities. In times of war and natural disaster, diverse religious groups unite in meeting human need. The entire religious spectrum participates in the battle against AIDS, violence, hunger, hate crimes, racism, and poverty. Interfaith dialogue is a mission activity in and of itself that is becoming a daily practice in our pluralist society. People of different faith traditions come together informally and formally with the goal of respectfully listening to and understanding one another. Dialogue promotes reconciliation and living together. It may or may not lead to evangelistic witness or mutual mission projects. Because of the uniqueness of Christ and the universality of the gospel, the church shares the message with all people. However, bold witness to people of other faiths requires humility and patience with great cultural and spiritual sensitivity to the readiness and receptivity of others and to the movement of God's Spirit in their lives.

How?

Often the church engages in legitimate mission activity, but proceeds in a way that contradicts the message of the gospel. Usually this is quite unintentional and because of one's culture. God's mission is one of proclamation, incarnation, prayer, action, fellowship, and dialogue. Jesus Christ not only demonstrated that mission is justice, evangelism, and service, but also showed the way, the attitude of mission. An exceptional PC(USA) document adopted by the General Assembly in 1991, *Turn to the Living God: A Call to Evangelism in Jesus Christ's Way,* shows that Jesus evangelized with inclusive servant love, by healing, through prayer, with urgency, through shared ministry and proclamation, and by living and calling people to a holy life.

In order to correct some of the terrible mistakes in mission and to emulate the incarnational model of God's Trinitarian mission, all service, justice, and evangelism today must be done in humility, with respect, in mutuality, and in solidarity.

Humility is the antidote to imperialism, colonialism, and paternalism. One-way mission that considers some to be superior

subjects and others to be inferior objects treated with condescension and pity is not *missio Dei*. Attitudes of arrogance and
unilateral actions of imposition or control do not befit God's mission. Most non-Anglo groups in the world feel anger and resent-
ment towards U.S. Anglos for our imperialism and attitudes of
superiority. We must truly demonstrate humble repentance and
seek to leave behind our wrong attitudes in mission. Evangelistic
encounters with the unreached and the unchurched, as well as
mission service and justice projects with other churches, cultures, and countries require what Bosch advocates in witness to
peoples of other faiths: "an admission that we do not have all the
answers and are prepared to live within the framework of penul-
timate knowledge . . . a bold humility—or a humble boldness."[23]

Respect for the dignity of every human being as a person created in God's image regardless of race, ethnicity, gender, sexual
orientation, economic status, ideology, and religion is fundamental in all mission sending and receiving. Especially in multicultural and cross-cultural settings, whether as hosts or as guests,
missioners should demonstrate respect for the culture and the
ideas of the other. Respect is the antidote to discrimination and
humiliation. We must recognize our unintentional "culture of
discrimination" and attitude of condescension, which often den-
igrate, blame, ignore, and alienate others. Mission in Christ's
way does not demean or humiliate anyone with charitable hand-
outs and cold, cruel treatment. It is anti-gospel to offer material
assistance at home or abroad without respecting the dignity of
others and entering into authentic, caring mutual relationships.
Mission partnerships are based on respect, risk, and trust.

Mutuality in mission is a two-way flow or exchange of giving
and receiving, speaking and listening, a relationship that is more
horizontal than vertical and does not create dependencies.
Mutual mission dignifies all persons and values the unique gifts,
abilities, and resources of all partners. Mutuality requires humility, patience, openness, honesty, true reciprocity—give and take.
Our greatest challenge is learning to listen, learn, receive, and
follow—to need the other—to give the other space and opportunity to speak and teach. We must be servants who seek to assist

and empower others, as well as receive what they have to offer us.

In mutual mission both partners are transformed, converted, evangelized. Gittins says, "Dialogue, born of mutual respect, mutual words, mutual listening, and mutual silence, is the fruit of 'mission in reverse.' "[24]

Solidarity is different from mutuality, which focuses on similarities. When we do not have similar experiences or are too different or distant to achieve mutuality, in solidarity we can still be with others and "affirm and embrace [our] incomprehensible differences as gifts to our common life."[25] It requires taking "seriously the ideas and experience of others on their own terms" and suspending our "own personal, cultural, and religious ideas and practices to listen for the experience and meanings of others."[26] Brazilian Claude E. Labrunie elucidates: "The Letter to the Philippians sought a word to express this mysterious action whereby God extends his hand, and it found the word 'emptiness': God emptied himself, became poor, in solidarity with the poor. If he became empty he lost his autonomy, his independence. God had to make himself a poor person." Solidarity focuses on affective identification and accompaniment, "to place ourselves *there,* to *accompany* the poor person. . . . To *sentir* (feel) with the poor person is to be one with her or him affectively and ethico-politically."[27] What would it look like for us to be in solidarity with people in Cuba, Iraq, or Somalia? With hurricane, tornado, or earthquake survivors? With people of other races, cultures, sexual orientations, or religions in our local communities?

Conclusion

My prayer is that God's Spirit, who was sent to comfort, encourage, teach, and empower the church for participation in God's mission, may unite the Presbyterian Church (U.S.A.) around the divine missional purpose and give us a new vision for two-way local-global mission through Christ and with Christ for the glory of God.

NOTES

1. David J. Bosch, *Transforming Mission: Paradigm Shifts in Theology of Mission* (Maryknoll, N.Y.: Orbis Books, 1991), 390.
2. Lucien Legrand, *Unity and Plurality: Mission in the Bible* (Maryknoll, N.Y.: Orbis Books, 1990), 141.
3. Darrell L. Guder, *Missional Church: A Vision for the Sending of the Church in North America* (Grand Rapids: Wm. B. Eerdmans Publishing Co., 1998), 83.
4. Bosch, *Transforming Mission*, 377.
5. Guder, *Missional Church*, 81.
6. Karl Barth, *Church Dogmatics*, IV/2, trans. G. W. Bromiley (Edinburgh: T. & T. Clark, 1958), 643–901.
7. Loren Mead, *Transforming Congregations for the Future* (Bethesda, Md.: Alban Institute, 1994), 64–65.
8. Guder, *Missional Church*, 81.
9. Lesslie Newbigin, *The Gospel in a Pluralist Society* (Grand Rapids: Wm. B. Eerdmans Publishing Co., 1989), 227.
10. Milton Coalter, John Mulder, and Louis Weeks, *Vital Signs: The Promise of Mainstream Protestantism* (Grand Rapids: Wm. B. Eerdmans Publishing Co., 1996), 91.
11. G. Thompson Brown, *Presbyterians in World Mission*, rev. ed. (Decatur, Ga.: CTS Press, 1995), 5.
12. John R. W. Stott, *Christian Mission in the Modern World* (Downers Grove, Ill.: InterVarsity Press, 1975), 30.
13. Anthony J. Gittins, *Bread for the Journey: The Mission of Transformation and the Transformation of Mission* (Maryknoll, N.Y.: Orbis Books, 1993), 16–17.
14. Ibid.
15. Howard Snyder uses this division in *Radical Renewal: The Problem of Wineskins Today* (Houston, Tex.: Touch Publications, 1996). Loren Mead in *Transforming Congregations* has a grid that enables people to place themselves in one of four mission quadrants. Ben Johnson in *New Day, New Church* (Decatur, Ga.: CTS Press, 1995) calls for the organization of a congregation into many mission groups with diverse foci.
16. Guder, *Missional Church*, 133.
17. Orlando Costas, *Christ outside the Gate* (Maryknoll, N.Y.: Orbis Books, 1982), 7.
18. Ibid.
19. Ibid., 192.
20. Jung Young Lee in *Marginality: The Key to Multicultural Theology* (Minneapolis: Fortress Press, 1995) interprets the incarnation as divine marginalization, Jesus as a paradigm of marginality, and the

church as a marginal people doing mission at the margins. Virgilio Elizondo, in *Galilean Journey* (Maryknoll, N.Y.: Orbis Books, 1983), compares the marginal experience of Jesus and Mexican Americans and the move from marginalization to new creation. One might conclude that mission is always done at the margins.

21. Bosch, *Transforming Mission*, 368.
22. Walter Brueggemann, *Biblical Perspectives on Evangelism* (Nashville: Abingdon Press, 1993), 71.
23. Bosch, *Transforming Mission*, 489.
24. Gittins, *Bread for the Journey*, 13.
25. Charles R. Foster, *Embracing Diversity: Leadership in Multicultural Congregations* (Bethesda, Md.: Alban Institute, 1997), 68.
26. Ibid., 68–69.
27. Roberto S. Goizueta, *Caminemos con Jesús: Toward a Hispanic/Latino Theology of Accompaniment* (Maryknoll, N.Y.: Orbis Books, 1995), 192, 194.

There's No Place like Home

Luke 15:17–24

James H. Logan, Jr.

Anybody that has ever traveled knows that there is no place like home. The pleasures this world has to offer cannot compare to the bliss of sleeping in your own bed, operating on your own schedule, and raiding your own refrigerator. Make no mistake about it, this world has much to offer, but its pleasures are but for a season (Heb. 11:25). The strategy of the enemy, however, is to convince you that what the world has to offer is far better than what you have at home, and that it is much to be desired. This strategy is employed freely and frequently against a people naive about the intention of the enemy to "rob, kill, and destroy (John 10:10)." The strategy is evident in every form of advertising, from billboards to magazines, radio, and television, and all of it beckons to you with screams almost too loud to ignore.

Many a well-intentioned, well-adjusted person has been caught by its allure. Drawn by promises of riches, freedoms, position, prominence, fame, and even love, the ranks of the beguiled steadily grow. Hoping to find the sweetness of freedom, they instead find the bitterness of slavery. Looking to prosper, they only fall into deeper debt. Believing they have finally found true love, they wind up used and abused.

Unfortunately, too many cut their ties when they leave the safe confines of home. Too many burn their bridges behind them when they celebrate their independence day, and as a result they are convinced that going home is the last thing they can do. While many people, because of the way in which they left home, probably cannot go back home (at least not in the same spirit that they left), I am so glad that God is always ready to welcome home the naive person gone astray.

The story of the prodigal son in the fifteenth chapter of Luke's Gospel vividly demonstrates just how welcoming our heavenly Father really is. It may be true that when you have messed up you cannot return to your earthly home, but there is nothing you can do that would stop your heavenly Father from lovingly waiting for you to come to your senses and return home. But just as many people do not try to return to their earthly homes, many do not attempt to return to their heavenly Father.

Having experienced the sweetness of the love of God, I find it difficult to understand why someone would not return home. Why would someone choose to remain in defeat when they can walk in victory? Why would someone choose to remain in poverty when they can experience prosperity? Why would someone willfully choose to remain a slave to all that is opposed to God when they can have freedom? The answer is one that many overlook, namely, the reality of our enemy, who blinds our eyes so that we cannot see, causing us to remain in our rebellion and believe that we are not welcome home.

Our text is a very familiar one. A wealthy man has two sons. The younger of the sons demands that he receive his inheritance before it is time, and ventures out into the world, where he squanders all his money in reckless living. Living the high life, he makes no provision for the future. So when hard times come, he goes bankrupt, and the so-called friends that he had bought are nowhere to be found. Having grown up in the lap of luxury and privilege, he winds up having to do the basest of menial tasks, slopping pigs. Finally he comes to a point of decision where he determines that it is far better to be a servant in his father's house than to live in the manner he has resorted to living now.

Though this text has been taught and preached repeatedly, I still see great insight in it. For there are many who, like the prodigal son in this story, have fallen into sin, not because someone mistreated them, not because they had become another statistic and fallen through the cracks, not because of someone else's negligence, but because of their own willful sin. This young man had no one but himself to blame for his predicament. He was the one who demanded that he receive his inheritance. He was the one who believed that the world was his oyster. He was the one who was "fronting," "living large," trying to be something he was not. Now, like the prodigal son, many people find themselves in a mess that they cannot seem to get out of, and they are too embarrassed and too ashamed to seek forgiveness and come home.

There are five timeless truths in this story that I believe are instructive for us today. First, the young man ended up in his condition because he had a desire to be independent. Second, he wound up in his predicament because of a desire to be looked up to and respected. Third, when the bottom of his life fell out, he was willing do almost anything just to survive, except that which could really save him. Fourth, shame and embarrassment kept him imprisoned and isolated from the one who could save him. Fifth and last, with his father he was always able to come home. Allow me to deal with them one at a time.

First, the young man ended up in his condition because he had a desire to be independent. Independence is a powerful desire for many people of all ages. Not many are willing to remain dependent on someone else their entire lives. The desire is especially strong for young people, who easily confuse their advancing age with wisdom. Many growing young people believe that they know more than their parents do. Great frustration and impatience set in among some young people as they struggle to balance obedience to the will of their parents with the strength of their drives and desires. The potential for conflict that drives wedges between parent and child is great, and without wise, mature parents many young people who stayed at home would be like the prodigal son who left home.

In my teens, I felt as though my parents were absolutely ignorant. I just knew that they knew nothing whatsoever about what it was like to be a teenager. I secretly suspected that they themselves had never even been teenagers. It was during this confusing time of my life that, frustrated and tired of having to bow to the dictates and commands of my parents, I determined to leave and go out on my own. I surmised that it was far more expedient for me to do what I thought best than to have to put up with the unrealistic expectations of parents I thought were out of touch with the real world. I thank God for my father, who very calmly pointed out that I had no job, no transportation, no place to live, and no income to get a place to live. Ever one to listen to reason, I quickly discerned that I was far better off at home than in the streets.

The prodigal son went through no such process of discernment. Filled with a desire to be independent from his father and convinced of his ability to care for himself, he went off to make his fortune. There is an appropriate time to leave the safe confines of home and make one's own way, but that time generally comes once we have been sufficiently prepared. Except in the case of physical, mental, or emotional conditions that necessitate continuing to be dependent, we were never intended to depend forever on our parents. Not so with God. In God we live and move and have our being. Separation from God is spiritual suicide, for without God we are nothing. Every time I have attempted to operate independent from God, I have wound up making a mess of my life. The prodigal son wound up in his condition because of a desire to be independent.

Second, he wound up in his predicament because of a desire to be looked up to and respected. Who doesn't want to be respected? Who doesn't wish to be looked up to? Most people are well able to live their lives without this desire becoming a driving force. This young man, however, was intent on "living large," living beyond his ability, just so he could portray an image of prosperity. Once a famine hit the country and his money was depleted, the reality of his foolish way of living became frighteningly manifest to the point that he was left working a demeaning job just to survive.

One does not have to leave home to wind up in the same predicament as the prodigal son. It is not at all unusual for people to become slaves to their jobs and limited by their paychecks because they have been living beyond their ability. Firms and ministries that counsel people on how to get out and stay out of debt are now big business because of the vast numbers of people who have fallen prey to the desire to be respected and looked up to. It is a fallacy to believe that money and possessions gain respect and cause people to admire you. Respect is gained not through the outward trappings of success, but through the integrity a person possesses. People do not even have to like you for who you are and what you believe, but they will respect you for the integrity of your faith and the consistency of your stand.

It is not clear from the text what precisely happened to the young man's money, except that he spent it in wild or riotous living. However, from the immaturity he demonstrated in leaving his father's house, we can surmise that he perhaps hoped that his money would buy him position, prominence, and prestige. But he was soon to discover, even as you and I discover, that the wages of sin is still death (Rom. 6:23). Where were those he had wined and dined? Where were all those who helped him spend his inheritance? Where were they when he was destitute? This young man wound up in his condition because of a desire to be respected and looked up to.

Third, when the bottom of his life fell out, he was willing to do almost anything just to survive, except that which could really save him. Perhaps you have never encountered a situation where it seems that everything that could possibly go wrong has gone wrong and there is seemingly no place where you can turn. It is not uncommon for us to pursue our personal agendas with no thought for the future. We enjoy the pleasures of sin that last for a season, while forgetting that the consequences can last a lifetime (Heb. 11:25). When we have tasted what the world has to offer and are now having to deal with the consequences, we encounter feelings of destitution that cause us to do whatever it takes to survive. In our city we see it every day. You cannot convince me that all the persons on the boulevard selling their bodies are doing so because they just want to. You cannot make me believe that drug-addicted persons break into houses, hold up businesses, sell off a loved one's possessions to support their habit just because they want to. These people find themselves in a predicament where they do what they do just to survive, and were it not for the grace of God, we would be doing the same thing.

The prodigal son was Jewish. Dietary laws forbade him from eating, touching, or even having anything to do with pigs. To touch or eat them was to make yourself ceremonially unclean. Certainly having to slop pigs was the lowest point to which this young man could sink. Then to recognize that with the money he was getting paid, he was not able to eat even as well as those pigs was an even greater insult. However, if he was to survive, it was a necessary sacrifice. It is easy to sit in polite Bible studies and friendly debates and talk about what we would never do. But until you come face to face with a situation that has you boxed in and locked down, you don't know what you will do if your very survival depends on it. This young man had the bottom of life fall out from under him, and if slopping pigs was what he had to do to survive, that was a price he was willing to pay. But thank God there was another option available for him: he could go home. But that option did not immediately occur to him, and that brings me to the fourth truth I see in this parable.

Fourth, shame and embarrassment kept him imprisoned and isolated from the one who could save him. When I read the parable of the prodigal son, I wonder why it took so long for the young man to decide that where he needed to be was at home. But then I remember that when I have stubbornly stepped out in rebellion, the most difficult thing for me to do was admit that I was wrong. This young man no doubt knew that he was wrong, but he could not bring himself to go home until he saw that the pigs he was slopping were better fed and better cared for than he was. It was at that point (v.17 says, "when he came to his senses") that he determined it would be better for him to be a servant in his father's house.

I wonder how many people are sleeping in the streets tonight because they are too ashamed to call home and admit that they were wrong. I wonder how many marriages have ended in divorce because one spouse was too ashamed and embarrassed to admit his or her error. I wonder how many friendships have lost their peace and harmony because of shame and embarrassment. There is no shame in admitting that you have made a bad decision. This young man could not get the help he needed until he determined to go home. Don't let shame and embarrassment keep you bottled up so that you cannot be helped, because when it comes to your heavenly Father, he is always standing waiting to receive you home.

Fifth and last, with his father he was always able to come home. I can understand the prodigal's hesitation as he came down the road. Certainly he wondered how his father would respond to him. After all, he had squandered all the money he had received. In his mind he was no longer worthy of sonship, and he was resigned to being little more than a servant. But what he did not know was that his father had been anxiously waiting for him to come home. So when this father saw his little boy coming down the road, while he was still at a distance, our text says that he began to run to him. When he got to his son, he kissed him, hugged him, and loved him, because the son who had been lost was now found. The son barely was able to get out his apology because of his father's exuberance.

That is the way it is with God. In the previous two parables in Luke 15 (the lost coin and the lost sheep), Jesus remarks that the exuberance in heaven over one sinner who has been found is great. God's love for his creation is so great that the heavenly host joins him in celebrating when another one of his creations comes to his or her senses and returns home. Regardless of how badly you have messed up, you can always come home. Your heavenly Father is waiting for you, looking down the road to see you come over the horizon, but the choice is yours to make. Coming home is an act of the will. You have to come to your senses, decide that you are weary of living the way you are, and come home.

It was the movie *The Wizard of Oz* that made recognizable the title of this message, "There's no place like home." Dorothy, swept by a hurricane into the land of Oz, desires to go home. The great wizard tells her to click the red heels of her shoes together three times while saying simultaneously, "There's no place like home, there's no place like home, there's no place like home." There is no place like home. But you won't get there by clicking your heels together. Rather, you will get there by getting up right in the midst of your mess, making up your mind that you are better off as a servant in your Father's house than where you are now, and going home. If you are ready to come home, *confess your sin, and ask God to forgive you, invite Jesus into your heart as your Lord and Savior, and begin to live the new life.*

When you discover how the enemy has lied to you, and you recognize the time you have lost living a lie, don't let guilt and shame bury you. You can always come home! Sin may appear very appealing, but when it captivates and enslaves you, you will shortly discover that there is no place like home. It is good to have friends and enjoy living the high life, but when your money has run out and your friends have deserted you, you will find that there is no place like home. You may have been rebellious, thumbed your nose at your family and the standards you were taught. But when your back is against the wall, you'll find that there is no place like home. Home is where your loving Father is waiting with open arms and receptive heart. Home is where a party is waiting in the wings to get started. Home is where you are absolutely loved and accepted regardless of what you have done or how you have messed up. Home is where the food is just right and the sheets smell right and you are surrounded with unconditional love.

Your heavenly Father is waiting for you today with open arms and the signs that you are welcome home. Will Thompson had it right when he wrote:

Softly and tenderly Jesus is calling, calling for you and for me;
Patient and loving, he's waiting and watching, watching for
you and for me.
Come home, come home, ye who are weary, come home;
Earnestly, tenderly, Jesus is calling—calling, "O sinner, come
home!"

Whatever you have done, in whatever condition you find yourself, make up your mind that there is no place like home, and come home to Jesus.

The Great Commission
or the Great Omission?
Matthew 28:16–20

James M. Singleton, Jr.

I n November of 1990 I visited India with a group on a mission study tour. Along with the impressive mission work that we saw, we were able to visit the most impressive architectural sight in India—the Taj Mahal. It is the most beautiful building that I have ever seen. Shah Jehan built it between 1632 and 1653 as both a mausoleum and a monument to his beloved wife, Mumtaz Mahal. A legend says that during the long process of building the Taj Mahal the shah often visited the construction site. During his inspections he regularly bumped into a dusty box that was often in his way. Finally one day he ordered, "Get rid of it!" The foreman began to protest, but the shah insisted, so they threw the box away. Only later did the shah discover that the box contained the body of the very woman the building was built to honor. The story may be only a legend, but it is certainly instructive.

It is very easy around a church to forget what and why we are building. From our beginnings in this country, Presbyterians have affirmed that evangelism was very important. The Presbyterian Church in the United States, the former southern Presbyterian church, once said in its *Book of Church Order* that "evangelism is the primary and urgent task of the church" (12.7-1). There was a time, prior to 1925, when that was true in that church body. It has been a long time, however, since local churches or the denomination or even Presbyterian individuals have acted as if evangelism was our "primary and urgent" task. At periods we have acted as if it was a "No Mission," as we have simply moved away from evangelism. Often evangelism has been a "Slow Mission," as we have done a little at a time. Most often evangelism has been simply an "O-Mission," something we have forgotten. Rarely has there been a sense of "Co-Mission," participating with God's Spirit in evangelism. We often say that evangelism is important, but we actually do little.

I am reminded of one of Søren Kierkegaard's parables that I heard years ago. A man was passing down the street when he noticed in the window of a shop a sign that read, "Pants Pressed Here." He paused and looked at his own pants. They were indeed quite wrinkled. He decided to enter the shop and have his pants pressed. So he walked up to the counter and began removing his pants. The clerk was quite shocked and asked, "What are you doing, sir?" The passerby said, "I want to have my pants pressed." The clerk replied, "Why would you seek that here?" The man replied, "Well, my pants are wrinkled, and you press pants, and I would like for you to press these pants." The clerk asked, "What would cause you to believe that we press pants?" The man replied, "You have a sign in your window that says you press pants." "Oh, you do not understand," said the clerk. "We do not press pants here; we paint signs here."

What about the church—do we do evangelism, or just paint signs?

To Whom the Charge Was Given

First, notice that there are eleven disciples to receive this Great Commission (Matt. 28:16). Eleven is a peculiar number here. Eleven is a good number for a football team, but we expect twelve here. There were twelve sons of Jacob, and thus twelve tribes of Israel. There are twelve gates into the New Jerusalem and twelve thrones around the throne of God. Twelve apostles had a nice ring to it. But suddenly there are eleven—Judas is gone and the number looks terribly incomplete. Dale Bruner writes, "The church that Jesus sends into the world is fallible, 'elevenish,' imperfect." [1]

Notice also that the disciples receiving this Great Commission have a marked ambivalence about Jesus. "When they saw him, they worshiped him; but some doubted" (Matt. 28:17). Doubt is quite common in the experience of the believer, yet some think that it ought not to be present among those standing before the risen Christ. Having doubt present as Christ gives his major mission thrust does seem a bit shaky.

This picture in Matthew is not far from the picture of the disciples when they receive a similar commission in Acts. There the same eleven disciples show their usual slowness of understanding. Their big question is about the kingdom. "Lord, is this the time when you will restore the kingdom to Israel?" (Acts 1:6). Because they used the word *restore*, it is likely that they held a view of the kingdom that was common in that day. The popular notion of the kingdom included a return for Israel to a time like that of David. That was a period marked by security and prosperity and independence. Throughout his earthly ministry Jesus taught about a different kind of kingdom, one that at root was "not from this world" (John 18:36). Following his death and resurrection, Jesus taught about the kingdom for forty days before his ascension (Acts 1:3). How disheartening it might have been for Jesus to hear the disciples' question after teaching them otherwise. The disciples still don't get it.

All this is merely one more evidence of the truth that Jesus is not particularly concerned about the ineptness of the recipients of this call. Is this not consistent with God's design? Paul wrote, "But we have this treasure in clay jars, so that it may be made clear that this extraordinary power belongs to God and does not come from us" (2 Cor. 4:7, NRSV). Is this not the lesson that we learn from the stories of Gideon, David, Ruth, Peter, and Mary? God does his best work with a group of Christians who have serious limitations.

In my previous presbytery, the Presbytery of the Inland Northwest, there were fifty churches. Certified Lay Pastors (CLP) provided pastoral leadership in ten of those congregations. The fastest growing church in that growing presbytery, with highest indicators related to evangelistic growth, was one of those small congregations led by a CLP. The CLP was the town mechanic. He did not have much professional training. There were lots of areas in which he did not feel qualified. But he truly received the Great Commission as his call and trusted God to guide the ministry.

Jesus is not at all worried about giving the Great Commission to a confused or misguided batch of believers—he still does it.

I called Delta Air Lines last spring to make reservations for a trip to Chicago. The woman who answered the phone replied, "Delta Air Lines. This is Josie Miller. May I help you." Hearing her voice and name, I dared to ask, "You are not the Josie Miller who once went to college in Memphis, are you?" She said haltingly, "Well, yes, I did." Then I introduced myself, and we were both shocked. I had not heard from Josie since 1980. Josie is the young woman who first invited me to allow the Holy Spirit to have control of my life in 1972 at a youth conference in Montreat, N.C. At that time Josie didn't know much about the Christian life. She just knew that it was true. In the words of the famous Indian evangelist, D. T. Niles, Josie was "one beggar showing another beggar where the bread was." She dared to invite me into a relationship with Jesus Christ that changed my life.

Many people think that we can be involved in God's mission to the world only when we move into the "graduate school" of Christian knowledge and experience. We feel that we are not knowledgeable enough, or bold enough, or friendly enough to share Jesus Christ with the world. But that is not true. A forgotten speaker once spoke a line I'll never forget—"God is more interested in our availability than our ability." Similarly, Elizabeth Elliot has said, "God never calls the equipped. Rather God equips the called."

God is not nervous about handing the Great Commission to us. God did not pick us for this project of evangelism because we were so good at it. God gave us a Co-Mission, promising his presence through the Holy Spirit. Can we trust in that presence?

The Great Commission Requires Risk

The directions that brought about this important meeting of Jesus and the disciples were apparently given by the risen Christ to some fearful women at the tomb—"Go and tell my brothers to go to Galilee; there they will see me" (Matt. 28:10). Thus we read that "the eleven disciples went to Galilee to the mountain where Jesus had told them to go" (v. 16). Would you have walked sixty miles in your grief on a tip from some women who claimed to have seen a dead man alive?

Biblical people often take risks. Abram and Sarai had to take risks—"Leave your home, kindred, and your land, and go to the land that I will show to you" (Gen. 12:1, paraphr.). Moses takes risks. Ruth and Naomi take risks. The women took risks by going early to the tomb. The book of Acts is full of risks. Many of us do not relish risks. When I try to be involved in evangelism I often see myself as the Don Knotts character from the movie *The Reluctant Astronaut*—someone full of fear and excuses.

We are usually willing to take risks because of passion. People climb mountains and paddle kayaks through rapids because of passion. People who are willing to share the faith with others are infected with a risky passion for the lost. Congregations who are willing to dare to do outreach do it because, in their union with Christ, they are infected with the same passion shown by Jesus when he said, "I have come to seek and save the lost" (Luke 19:10).

Yet many in our tradition hate to take the risks of verbally sharing our faith. We would rather let our actions do the talking. Years ago Marcel Marceau, the great mime, was interviewed by a Detroit paper. He was asked, "Is it more difficult to be a mime or an actor?" Marceau answered, "To be a mime is more difficult. An actor always has the words to explain his action. But the action of a mime has to be so clear and precise that no one mistakes what he is doing." I am afraid that those who witness only by their actions are rarely that clear.

In Edward Gibbon's classic, *The History of the Decline and Fall of the Roman Empire*, his chapter on the causes of the rapid spread of Christianity is quite insightful. He describes the growth of a faith in an environment that was very hostile to it. There was in that growth a factor that he could not deny, though he himself was unsympathetic to it. Gibbon believed that the cause of the rapid growth was that each new convert considered it as his or her sacred duty "to diffuse among his friends and relations the inestimable blessing which he had received."[2] That was risk inspired by passion.

"Go Therefore and Make Disciples of All Nations"

Notice first the outward thrust of the call. In many ways it was a new concept. In the Old Testament the missional perspective was one of concern for the nations. God made them, and they will come and bow down to him. But there was little sense of mission to the nations by going out to win them (see Ps. 96:3). There were visions of a pilgrimage of the nations to Mount Zion (e.g., Isa. 2:2–3). The direction is a centripetal activity—coming to the center. Only in the New Testament is the centripetal missionary consciousness replaced by a centrifugal missionary activity.[3]

The direction was no longer "come hither," but "go forth." In a similar passage in Acts the disciples are called to be witnesses first to "Jerusalem," then to Judea and Samaria, then "to the ends of the earth" (Acts 1:8).

Are we "going" into the lives of other people for God? Personally are we going? Are our churches taking the word out? Or are we isolating ourselves in a holy huddle?

"Make Disciples"

The other notable feature in this verse is the call to make disciples. That is ultimately a work of the Spirit that comes as a result of our union with Christ. It is a much more comprehensive concept than merely making a convert. It involves the process of becoming like Christ.

Lloyd C. Douglas, in his marvelous historical novel *The Robe*, has a character named Marcellus, who became a disciple of Jesus. Marcellus wrote to his lover in Rome, named Diana, about his conversion. She replied, "What I feared was that it might affect you. It is a beautiful story. Let it remain so. We don't have to do anything about it, do we?"[4]

We are called to remember to call people to become disciples of Jesus—to live in thankful response to the good news of Jesus. We are not called to make converts. Neither are we called to make church members. The call is to make disciples.

"I Will Be with You"

The overarching promise of this passage is the presence of Jesus Christ in our call to mission. Ultimately we simply have the joy of participating in "God's mission to the world." We do not always remember that. Too often, whatever we do, we try to do alone. The call is to remember that Jesus intended for this to be a Co-Mission, joining Spirit and church in the task of making disciples. Thus, we pray for and look for God's participation in his mission to the world. The joyful surprise is that God wants us to be involved with him.

A popular story that provides a wonderful picture of that combination comes from the lore surrounding Ignace Paderewski, the great pianist and one-time prime minister of Poland. A woman wanted her five-year-old son to practice his piano more. She thought that if she took the child to see and hear Paderewski, her son would be inspired and want to practice. So she bought a pair of tickets on the front row. On the night of the performance, they arrived a few minutes early. The woman saw a friend seated on the second row, and she turned to talk. The son was unwatched. He knew why he was there—because mom wanted him to practice. He saw an empty piano before him, and there was nothing to do. So he thought he would practice and make mother happy. He climbed up onto the stage and began to practice. People giggled, and the mother turned to see why. In her horror she saw her child on the bench. Her son was playing "Twinkle, Twinkle, Little Star." Just as she tried to get up to retrieve her child, applause began all around her. Paderewski was coming onto the stage. With his left hand he found a bass part for "Twinkle, Twinkle." With his right hand he played a beautiful obbligato part on the theme. He simply whispered in the child's ear, "Don't stop, keep playing." Master and child made beautiful music together.

This call of Christ to make disciples does not need to be a Great Omission. Together let it be the Great Co-Mission.

NOTES

1. Frederick Dale Bruner, *Matthew*, vol. 2 (Waco, Tex.: Word Publishing, 1990), 1090.
2. Edward Gibbon, *The History of the Decline and Fall of the Roman Empire* (Philadelphia: Porter & Coates, n.d.), vol. 1, 515.
3. See Johannes Blauw, *The Missionary Nature of the Church* (London: Lutterworth Press, 1962), 34, 54, 66.
4. Lloyd C. Douglas, *The Robe* (New York: Pocket Books, 1958), 496.